JOHN-PAUL FLINTOFF is an author, writer and broadcaster. He trained as an investigative reporter, worked for several years at the *Financial Times*, then for the *Sunday Times*, and has written for many other newspapers and magazines around the world. His work has won several awards, and has led directly to changes to UK government policy. For more, see www.flintoff.org

THE SCHOOL OF LIFE is dedicated to exploring life's big questions: *How can we fulfil our potential? Can work be inspiring? Why does community matter? Can relationships last a lifetime?* We don't have all the answers, but we will direct you towards a variety of useful ideas – from philosophy to literature, psychology to the visual arts – that are guaranteed to stimulate, provoke, nourish and console

How to Change the World
John-Paul Flintoff

MACMILLAN

First published 2012 by Macmillan
an imprint of Pan Macmillan, a division
of Macmillan Publishers Limited

Pan Macmillan,
20 New Wharf Road, London N1 9RR
Basingstoke and Oxford
Associated companies throughout the world
www.panmacmillan.com

ISBN 978-1-4472-0232-5

9 8 7 6 5 4 3

A CIP catalogue record for this book is
available from the British Library.

Cover designed by Marcia Mihotich
Text design and setting by seagulls.net
Printed and bound by CPI Group (UK) Ltd,
Croydon, CR0 4YY

Visit www.panmacmillan.com to read
more about all our books and to buy
them. You will also find features,
author interviews and news of any
author events, and you can sign up for
e-newsletters so that you're always first
to hear about our new releases.

'Imperfection is an end. Perfection is only an aim'
– Ivor Cutler

Contents

I. Introduction

If you had the chance, would you change the world? Of course you would. There are plenty of things that you would change right now, if you were given a magic wand.

After all, the world is desperately in need of improvement. So much so that sometimes we lie awake at night, turning over for hours on end as we worry about it. During the day, we huff and curse at the many smaller things that seem wrong. And in sunnier moments we allow ourselves to dream, conjuring parallel worlds that seem entirely delightful.

But whatever our disposition, we often conclude that to change the world would be hard work, if not impossible. And so we don't even try.

That's a shame, because actively creating change brings benefits for ourselves as individuals, too: we discover deeper reserves of empathy and opportunities to be creative, and we can cultivate a habit of fearlessness. Better still, it turns out that changing the world produces a deep, lasting sense of satisfaction – not only when we've 'finished', as if that were possible, but at each step along the way.

If you have read even this far, you are already interested in changing the world. You may also be confident that you can do something. But not everybody will share that confidence. In which case, it's as well to remember that the ideas set down in this book are validated by ancient wisdom and the latest in scientific research. And they're not merely theoretical, but grounded in historical fact: they've been shown to work. By the time you have finished reading, you should be better equipped to make change, and also more determined to do so.

To back up the analysis, the book is full of anecdotes, from across history and around the world. Some of these stories are of great historical significance, but I have also included stories from my own life, or from the lives of people I know, precisely in order to show that changing the world is not only the business of 'great souls' like Gandhi, Mother Teresa or Nelson Mandela.

I make no apology for using these personal stories. On the contrary, it would be shameful to argue that everybody is capable of making change if I didn't mention some of my own experiences. They are not intended to seem outstanding: they just happen to be mine. Feminist theory teaches that 'the personal is the political', and if that's the case then the evidence to prove it will almost by definition appear rather unremarkable. But it's evidence all the same, and shows that the small, everyday actions of 'ordinary' individuals have the potential to be world-changing.

The point of this book is not only to offer a few intellectual propositions for you to absorb. We learn best by doing, and a book like this is useful only if you put it into practice. As you are reading, think how it might apply to your own situation.

And then try it.

II. How to Start to Make a Change

1. Overcoming Defeatism

How can I, one individual in a world of billions, hope to change anything? There are many reasons why this kind of defeatist question comes so easily to us. They include the way we have been brought up, a lifetime of putting up with things that frustrate or dismay us, and painful memories of failed attempts to Do Something.

But the fact remains that we are all making a difference all the time. The real problem is that if we're only affecting things unconsciously then we are probably not producing the effect we would wish for.

Some people may find it hard to believe they are making a difference all the time. In which case, it may help to abandon the global perspective for a moment and zoom in to our daily human interactions – in which we spend every moment either deciding what must happen next or going along with somebody else's ideas. Either way, our actions are all purposeful, and all produce effects. Our day-to-day lives are hardly the stuff of history, you might argue. Certainly not compared with Julius Caesar invading Britain, Genghis Khan sacking Baghdad and Christopher Columbus discovering America. That's how many people understand history. 'The history of the world is but the biography of great men,' wrote Thomas Carlyle. But the 'great man' theory of history has been on its way out for years. Nowadays, we recognize that those men couldn't have done what they did on

their own. And we identify historical significance in hitherto overlooked episodes.

The Russian novelist Leo Tolstoy was one of the first to observe
that history should more accurately be considered to consist of the
combined effect of the many small things that ordinary individuals do
every day: 'An infinitely large number of infinitesimally small actions'.

As Tolstoy saw it, we are making history from the moment we
get up in the morning till we go to bed at night. And it's not only the
things we *do* that make history, it's also the things we don't do. That's
obvious when you think about, say, voting in an election or not. But
taken to its logical conclusion it also goes to show that we are making
a difference even *after* going to bed: because we are sleeping instead
of, say, working all night on some earthshaking political manifesto,
or patrolling the streets to feed the homeless.

And that's fine, by the way: we all need to sleep. But Tolstoy's
insight requires us to recognize that we are *all* responsible for the
way things are. 'We are each absolutely essential, each totally irre-
placeable,' says the Native American activist Leonard Peltier. 'Each
of us is the swing vote in the bitter election battle now being waged
between our best and our worst possibilities.'

And yet the old idea ingrained in us throughout school, that history
is about the actions of dominant individuals, is hard to shake off.
Indeed, it seems that, even in democracies, it is positively encouraged.

On the twentieth anniversary of the Berlin Wall coming down,
'world leaders' flew in to Germany to deliver speeches to the listen-
ing masses.

It was striking that they came to take credit for this particular historical event, because world leaders had had very little to do with the Wall's collapse. In reality, the barrier between East and West Berlin was pulled down because many ordinary Berliners did something very small. Having witnessed 'people power' effecting significant change in several neighbouring countries, and following massive protests elsewhere in East Germany, they merely turned up at the border to see what was going on. Soldiers at the control post, overwhelmed and likewise conscious of what had recently happened in neighbouring countries, opened the way for them to cross freely from one side of the city to the other. Soon after, the wall having ceased to be an effective barrier, it was pulled down. The fact that 'world leaders' took the credit does not diminish the achievement, but does suggest that, when changing the world, we can't necessarily expect recognition for it.

When we talk about the ways the world frustrates us, we often reach for terms like 'the system' or 'the status quo', and, shrugging, complain that we are powerless. We might do this if a great wall were built through the middle of our city, preventing us from seeing friends and relatives, but also in the face of much lesser hardships. Let's imagine for a moment that we want to hold a street party, but find ourselves obstructed by petty civic regulations that were drawn up for entirely other purposes: we give up. With terms as abstract as 'the system' and 'the status quo', it can be hard to see our own complicity in the problem. The truth is that we have a choice. We could try to change the regulations that obstruct us, or even disregard them. The choice is entirely ours.

The Berlin Wall: when enough people came, the soldiers had to let them through.

To put this into terms that a child could understand: imagine for a moment that the status quo is a powerful king. Shut your eyes and try to picture him. How do you know he's a powerful king? Is it because he has a big crown? A golden throne? No, those only tell us that he's king. How do we know that he's *powerful*? It's the other people nearby, lying flat on their faces and trembling. It's *their* behaviour that makes the king seem powerful, not his. If they got up off their faces, turned their backs and started to tell jokes, or smoke cigarettes, or have a snooze, the same imaginary king, with the same big crown and golden throne, would no longer seem very powerful at all. Now imagine the powerful king is an actor on stage, and that those prostrate before him are also actors. An actor lying flat on his face before a seemingly powerful king knows that there is an alternative: at any moment, he could get up and do something else, with tremendous effect. In real life we also have the ability to step outside of our normal role and do something else, but we often forget it – if we ever knew.

This is partly because conventional wisdom, and the kind of kings-and-queens-and-presidents history taught to children from a young age, hold that power is vested at the top. Like the Wizard of Oz, parents and teachers encourage children to believe that they, and other 'authority' figures, are all-powerful. As we grow into adults, we are encouraged to believe that employers and governments are all-powerful too. And for as long as we believe it, they truly are.

It may seem bizarre to dress up this everyday business as turning our backs on a powerful king, but many people around the world do indeed feel powerless in the face of bullies – whether they are rulers or employers or indeed friends or family – and it can be liberating to remember that, whatever the consequences, obedience is entirely our own choice.

Tolstoy was baffled that people did not recognize this. He couldn't understand why ordinary Russian peasants, having joined the Tsar's army, were prepared to kill other Russian peasants, perhaps even their fathers and brothers – just because the Tsar told them to. Troubled by this and other questions of social justice, Tolstoy gave up the fashionable life and retired to his farm. While he was there, he was contacted by a young, politically active Indian man then living in South Africa. Tolstoy wrote back, and subsequently published his 'A Letter to A Hindu'.

Describing the subjugation of India by the British East India Company, Tolstoy wrote: 'A commercial company enslaved a nation comprising two hundred millions. Tell this to a man free from superstition and he will fail to grasp what these words mean. What does it mean that thirty thousand people, not athletes, but rather weak and ordinary people, have enslaved two hundred millions of vigorous, clever, capable, freedom-loving people? Do not the figures make it clear that . . . the Indians have enslaved themselves?'

The young Hindu Tolstoy wrote to was Mohandas K. Gandhi, who had a privileged background like him. But Gandhi had felt for himself the humiliating effect of injustice when he was thrown off a train in South Africa for having dark skin. From that moment on, he devoted himself to fighting oppression. Moving back to his native India, then under the control of Great Britain, he started a non-violent campaign for freedom.

Gandhi emphasized the importance of a change of will as a prerequisite for a change in patterns of obedience and cooperation. There was a need for (1) a psychological change away from passive submission to self-respect and courage, (2) recognition by the subject that his assistance makes the regime possible and (3) the building of a determination to withdraw cooperation and obedience. Gandhi felt that these changes could be consciously influenced, and deliberately set out to bring them about:

> My speeches are intended to create 'disaffection' as such, that people might consider it a shame to assist or cooperate with a government that has forfeited all title to respect or support.
>
> The moment the slave resolves that he will no longer be a slave, his fetters fall. He frees himself and shows the way to others. Freedom and slavery are mental states. Therefore the first thing to say to yourself: 'I shall no longer accept the role of a slave. I shall not obey orders as such but shall disobey them when they are in conflict with my conscience.'

Naturally, the British were outraged. Still today, some people find it hard to accept the legitimacy of civil disobedience. The law must be respected, they might say. But to take that position is to argue that, once Hitler's regime came to power, it was the duty of all Germans to obey it completely. Few today believe that. On the contrary, most believe that under certain conditions, disobedience and defiance are absolutely justified.

The daily reality is that obedience is never universally practised by the whole population. Many people sometimes disobey the law, or break lesser regulations, and some people do so frequently. Some do it for selfish reasons and some do it for nobler ones. Dramatic instances of mass disobedience are only more visible evidences of this general and everyday truth.

If you have picked up this book because you already have an idea for changing the world, involving, say, the manufacture of a cheap and comfortable shoe, you may be a little alarmed by the turn things have taken: Gandhi's talk of mental slavery, and my own reference to Hitler. What has this to do with you? Well, it's true that we do not need to believe we are slaves, or live in a dictatorship, in order to take part in changing the world. We need only to believe that something is seriously wrong (the cost, and discomfort, of shoes currently available?) and to resolve that we are not willing to put up with it any longer.

All the same, I mention Nazi Germany for a purpose. I want to argue that even if you think your efforts may not be decisive, it's imperative that you try.

Sceptics often say that ordinary people's non-violent political efforts could not have defeated the Nazis. Are they right? Hypotheticals can never be proven, one way or the other. Rather than get bogged down in debate about whether non-violence 'might have' beaten the Nazis, Gene Sharp encourages us instead to consider how the Nazis actually *were* opposed non-violently, both within Germany and in occupied countries.

An academic who has held tenure at Oxford and Harvard, Sharp published his first work in 1960, with a foreword by Albert Einstein. In the first volume of his magnum opus, *The Politics of Non-violent Action*, Sharp demands that we remove our blinkers and recognize that political power is our own power – and that it does not reside only in the ballot box. In that book and elsewhere, Sharp provides a stunningly comprehensive account of non-violent resistance to the Nazis, often overlooked by military historians.

There are too many instances to list here, but the following paragraphs hint at the variety of approaches.

When prisoners started to escape from a Polish prison, a young woman telegrapher risked her life by simply failing to send a message calling for reinforcements.

In Norway, citizens looked right through German soldiers, as if they didn't exist, and refused to sit next to them on public transport. If this sounds mild, it seriously rattled the Germans: it became an offence to stand, on trams, if there was a seat available. Who could have imagined that Nazi morale was so fragile?

In Denmark, the king wore a yellow star in sympathy with Jews who were forced to wear them. When Danish officials were instructed to round up Jews for deportation, they let the information get out, allowing plenty of time for people to go into hiding. Many Danes simply disregarded the Nazi-imposed curfew, staying out at night as long as they liked.

In Holland, some 25,000 Jews successfully went into hiding, many of them with help from non-Jews.

In Germany, a group of non-Jewish citizens protested publicly after their Jewish husbands and wives were taken away. The protest took place at the height of the war, and in the centre of Berlin. Incredibly, the protesters got what they wanted: their spouses were returned home and remained safe for the rest of the war.

Twice, German field marshals walked out on Hitler during meetings.

Doctors who disliked the regime exempted young men from military service. (They came to be known as 'Guten Tag' doctors, because that was how they greeted patients, instead of saying 'Heil Hitler'.)

German musicians undermined the prohibition on playing American jazz by making up German names for the tunes they liked.

The best-known opposition to Hitler was organized by the White Rose Group, which produced anti-Nazi propaganda distributed by post to households across the country, chosen at random from the phone book. The leaflets started to appear in 1942, when the war was still going well for Germany. 'We will not be silent!' one read. 'We are your bad conscience!' The leaflets were found all over the country. Nobody suspected that the White Rose consisted of a tiny group of friends in Munich. Their last leaflet was smuggled out of Germany and millions of copies were dropped over Germany from Allied planes. News even reached the concentration camps. 'When we heard what was happening in Munich,' one inmate later recalled, 'we embraced each other and applauded. There were, after all, still human beings in Germany.'

Some of these actions are almost laughably small: playing American jazz! But as we shall see, even the smallest act of subversion has the potential to inspire others.

If it hadn't been for these minor setbacks, Hitler's regime might have been even worse than it actually was. To put it another way: if more people had dared to resist, the Nazis worst outrages might have been prevented.

To say this is not merely to pass judgement on people living long ago. It's to challenge ourselves, right now. Because it's easy to imagine that we'd have acted boldly if we'd been in Germany at the time.

But the honest question to ask is whether there is anything we should be doing *today*, about something that is going on right now. To ask ourselves if there have been times when we knew we should have done something, but didn't, and to remember how awful that felt. And then resolve to do everything we can to avoid feeling that way again.

2. What Drives Us?

Some people may be lucky. They will know exactly what they want to change. But for many it's uncertain. There are so many problems, and so many ways to deal with them. Surprisingly often, we find ourselves impaled on a paradox: we desperately want to do something, but have no idea what it may be.

To look for inspiration to the great breakthroughs of the past does not always help, because one of the most common effects of success is to be taken for granted: what once seemed impossible looks ordinary after it's been accomplished. For the same reason, the role taken by particular individuals has a tendency, with hindsight, to seem inevitable, or pre-ordained. We find it hard, for instance, to imagine Gandhi leading a life of inoffensive middle-class respectability. But he might have done. He didn't, because he found that other things mattered more to him than the conventional legal career for which he had trained.

We too, if we hope to change the world, must try to understand what drives us. In particular, we need to understand whether to follow our interests, or a sense of duty.

Historically, many people tried to follow the teachings of religious authorities, perhaps in the hope of a better afterlife. Immanuel Kant promoted the idea of duty for its own sake, regardless of reward in heaven or punishment in hell. He suggested that we act morally only when we have put aside all motives stemming from our desires or inclinations. But this can lead to rigid fanaticism, as the philosopher Peter Singer points out in his book *How Are We To Live?*

> Before his trial, the Nazi Adolf Eichmann suddenly declared with great emphasis that he had lived his whole life according to Kant's moral precepts and especially the Kantian definition of duty . . . on occasions he felt sympathy for the Jews he was sending to the gas chambers but because he believed one should do one's duty unaffected by sympathy he steadfastly stuck to his duty. Another Nazi, Heinrich Himmler, told SS troops assigned to kill Jews that they were called upon to fulfil a 'repulsive duty' and that he would not like it if they did such a thing gladly.

The eighteenth-century philosopher David Hume opposed Kant's view. He believed that every reason for doing anything has to connect with some desire or emotion if it is to influence our behaviour. If Hume is right, the only way to answer the question, 'What should I do?' is by first asking, 'What do I *want* to do?'

But there's a danger here, too: we might want to pursue narrowly selfish interests. This is fine, up to a point, but there comes a time in most people's lives when that no longer seems adequate – often when we become truly conscious of our own mortality.

For centuries, people used the awareness of death deliberately to focus the mind on living well while we can. A story found in many variants across medieval Europe told of three proud, handsome and rich young courtiers riding in the forest, where they encountered three rotting corpses. The corpses said to the men: 'As you are now, so once were we. As we are now, so shall you be.' One can readily imagine how such an incident might get the young men thinking, because something similar happens in real life. People who recover from near death say the experience is character-building, and gives a clearer perspective on what is really important. The Buddha had a similar insight. After growing up in a palace, protected from the problems of the world, he went out one day and saw an old person, a man grievously ill, and a dead body. He asked his chariot driver whom these things happened to and was stunned by the answer: 'To everyone, my lord.' Buddhists acknowledge the great value of these dreadful sights by calling them Heavenly Messengers – because they spur us to seek awakening.

According to the philosopher Stephen Batchelor, in his study of Buddhism and existentialism, *Alone with Others*, we all 'know' that we must die, and that the things we leave will eventually fade or crumble away. But most of us habitually behave as though the opposite were true – as if we were immortal. And we refuse to accept our cosmic insignificance because to focus on it can be terrifying: our entire world is just one planet circling round one star in a galaxy that contains about 300,000 million stars and is itself one of several million galaxies. The sun will eventually grow cold, and life on earth will come to an end, but the universe will continue, utterly indifferent.

Authentic existence means accepting our inevitable death, and cosmic insignificance – and deciding to live purposefully all the same.

Jean-Paul Sartre conveyed our situation in a paradox: 'Man is condemned to be free', while Albert Camus likened our lives to the hard existence of Sisyphus, obliged by the Greek gods to push a

'As you are now, so once were we. As we are now, so shall you be.'
A vivid sense of our own mortality does tend to concentrate the mind.

heavy rock uphill then watch it roll back down, again and again for all eternity.

Today, as Singer has pointed out, the assertion that life is meaningless is no longer regarded as a shocking discovery. It's repeated every day by bored adolescents. But that doesn't mean we can't do something meaningful within it, on our own terms. Even Sisyphus, Camus believed, can find satisfaction if he really tries: 'There is no fate that cannot be surmounted'.

But it can only be surmounted if we confront it directly. If we do that, we find the courage to move through to empowerment and growth. That's confirmed by the psychiatrist Chris Johnstone. In his work with alcoholics and addicts, he makes the obvious but necessary point that if we forbid ourselves to talk negatively about something, 'We block the awareness of grievances that need an airing as a prelude to dealing with them'. Johnstone describes our grievance as a 'call to adventure' that sends us out into the world to make things better, just as the 'heavenly messengers' set the Buddha on his path to enlightenment. Many children's stories start with something similar – a catastrophic turn of events, or a shocking revelation, that pushes the unwilling hero into the world to right wrongs before returning home triumphant.

There is something counter-intuitive about welcoming the thing that makes us unhappy. But if you don't truly accept that there's a problem, you might lack the determination necessary to fix it. This is particularly obvious when people who are worried about, say, climate change ask experts whether we are going to 'make it'. If the expert says yes, people lapse back into business as usual. If the expert says no, everybody falls into despair. Neither attitude will make change happen.

Studies have shown that inducing fear about the way things are, without simultaneously giving people a sense of purpose, can actually suppress their immune system – it will make them unwell. The psychiatrist Viktor Frankl based his life's great work on this insight, which he saw for himself as a prisoner in Nazi concentration camps. The prisoner who had lost faith in his future was doomed. In his book *Man's Search for Meaning*, Frankl quotes Nietzsche: 'He who has a "why" to live for can bear almost any "how".' If we find a reason, we can overcome anything.

> Man is not fully conditioned and determined but rather determines himself whether he gives in to conditions or stands up to them. Man does not simply exist but always decides what his existence will be, what he will do in the next moment. By the same token, every human being has the freedom to change at any instant . . . One of the main features of human existence is the capacity to rise above [our] conditions, to grow beyond them.

The search for meaning must always come before the pursuit of happiness, Frankl insists, as we must have a reason to be happy. Once the reason is found, one becomes happy automatically. But when Frankl talked about meaning, he didn't only mean some grand, ultimate purpose, of the sort that might appear on our gravestone. He meant the potential meaning inherent and dormant in every situation we ever encounter. 'The perception of meaning boils down to becoming aware of what can be done about a given situation.'

In recent years, his suggestion has been confirmed by the 'positive psychology' movement led by Martin Seligman. Using scientific methods, Seligman and his colleagues compared the experiences of groups of people enjoying different types of pleasure. One group was sent out to experience sheer hedonism – say, having a foot massage or eating chocolate. Another group was asked to do things that they felt were 'meaningful'. The satisfaction enjoyed by this second group was shown to be both deeper and longer lasting. Several individuals reported that the 'afterglow' didn't only improve their day but also the way they felt about themselves generally.

Changing the world, in other words, feels good – better than pursuing narrowly selfish interests, better even than having your feet massaged while you eat chocolate.

The particular 'meaningful' actions taken are not ultimately important in this context. Others, doing the same things but without stopping to think *why*, would not have shared the sense of satisfaction. To give a simple example: your neighbour is unwell and you take their dog for a walk; you might do so because you genuinely *want* to help them at this difficult time, or you might do it resentfully. The first will make you feel good, the second won't.

This explains how it can be that, if changing the world consists only of everyday actions, some people are actively doing it and others are not. There's a distinction to be made between people who are changing the world merely by existing and others who seek *deliberately* to make a difference: only the person who actively seeks to make change truly understands that there is a choice to be made about how we lead our lives, and can observe clearly the effect they are having. To change the world is to have a sense of purpose, and

Is this a fun way of helping your neighbour, or a chore?

that's something we can all cultivate. Just ask yourself, every so often: 'Why am I doing this?'

Questions like this help us to find what Chris Johnstone (echoing Hume) calls 'the want behind the should'. We won't be motivated to change the world if doing so threatens to be a dreary obligation – but if we can find ways to do it that overlap with the things we most enjoy in life, we're more likely to stick at it.

When we are immersed in activities we love, we are living by our intrinsic values. These are not the general values that everybody pays lip service to but a collection of ideals that are important to us individually – values that get us out of bed in the morning, or make us turn off the TV if something upsets us. Many people will share some of our values, but taken as a whole they are uniquely ours.

One way to grasp your own values is to ask yourself: what do I think of as a good life, in the fullest sense of that term? What kind of life do I truly admire, and what kind of life do I hope to be able to look back on? To be more specific, write a list of things to accomplish by the time you die. What steps are needed to make them happen?

You might also try writing ten different answers to the question 'Who Am I?' Find the reason you are excited by each answer, and see if you can find a pattern. Then put the answers in order, from favourite to least favourite. Everybody will do this differently, but it's likely that most people's answers will include relationships (I'm a father, a son, a husband, a brother, a friend, a neighbour, and so on), ways in which they have made a living, and outside interests. It takes work to determine what we find exciting in each case, but it's worthwhile because it teaches us something about ourselves that we might never previously have considered.

A similar exercise involves making a note of events or relationships that have made you feel truly alive in the recent or distant past, and then (just as important) trying to analyse why. Answer the question honestly – don't assume that a 'worthy' answer is required. For instance, if you happened to feel truly alive playing golf, write that down. Then ask yourself: was it because you like being outdoors, or because you are competitive at sport, or because you like the opportunity to chat with people, or some other reason? Once you have identified the reason, ask yourself why you enjoy *that*. Write down the answer, and keep breaking down the pleasure you derive from the activity until you get to the 'ultimate' reason why you enjoy it. Then ask what other things you could do that would lead to the same kind of ultimate satisfaction. The exercise might go something like this:

> *What do I enjoy?* Playing golf
> *Why?* Because I like seeing my friends
> *Why?* Because I enjoy open, unhurried opportunities to chat with friends
> *Why?* Because I am a sociable person, and like to find out what makes people tick

From this you could conclude that you might find satisfaction volunteering to talk to people, perhaps as a trained counsellor. It might involve a bit of work, but trying to change the world for the better in that area could make you just as happy as a round of golf.

Another thing we might do is look back at times when we have made a difference, no matter how small, and try to remember what that felt like.

Standing in front of a tank: to focus too much on this kind of
monumental struggle can be misleading.

It's imperative to actually do the exercises. Reading them and skipping on won't help at all. Only by doing the exercises can you hope to find a better sense of the things that give your life meaning.

This helps to determine how we should act, because the question we are looking at is not 'What is the meaning of life?', but 'How can I make my life meaningful?' And the answer to that requires action.

To focus too much on monumental struggles – such as that of the lone Chinese student who, in Tiananmen Square in 1989, went with his shopping bags to block a column of tanks – can be misleading. Ethics appear in our lives in much more ordinary, everyday ways. The Victorian artist and writer John Ruskin once asked why we give medals to people who, in a moment and without much thought, save somebody's life, but we give no medal to people who devote years to bringing up a child.

Even the mundane can acquire grandeur if it's held in a wider perspective. A researcher once asked men working with stone what they were doing. One said his job was to square off the stones and move them. Another said he was working to provide for his wife and children. A third, while conscious that he was doing both those things, said he was building a magnificent cathedral, for people to worship in long after he'd gone. Each of them was doing great work, but only one recognized how great it was. We can even impose a kind of grandeur on everyday parenting, of the sort Ruskin described, if we see it as the work of a 'good ancestor', striving to pass on the best of our distant forebears to people as yet unborn.

The novelist and philosopher Iris Murdoch insisted that leading a good life involves not only occasionally making grand gestures, whether standing in front of tanks or giving blood (a less dramatic way to save lives). 'The exercise of our freedom is a small piecemeal business which goes on all the time, and not a grandiose leaping about unimpeded at important moments.' It's about the way we conduct ourselves from one moment to the next.

It's also, crucially, about how we observe the world around us. Murdoch believed we should cultivate a kind of 'mindfulness'. By making a habit of focusing our attention on everyday things that are valuable or virtuous, we hone our ability to act well at decisive moments. 'Anything that alters consciousness in the direction of unselfishness will do,' she wrote.

And that's because, if we are really interested in changing the world, we have to put other people first. Every attitude we assume, every word we utter, and every act we undertake establishes us in relation to others. We may be alone in the realms of our private thoughts, perceptions and feelings, but the world we want to change consists of other people.

And this gives us an important clue as to where we might find the meaning we are looking for: in helping others. Because if we are not doing that, we are still pursuing narrowly selfish interests.

3. Some Thoughts on Strategy

Having understood what drives us, we should be in a better position to choose between the many issues that deserve our attention. One way to do this might be to write a list, putting the issues into an order of priorities. Perhaps like this:

- War
- Poverty
- Environmental degradation
- Famine
- Political corruption . . .

And so on. But each person's list will be different, sometimes radically so. The issues that worry somebody in one part of the world may not bother another person elsewhere (even if they 'should'). For example, it is hard to imagine making famine our mission if we have no experience of it, and do not even know where a famine is to be found. As the last chapter explored, if we're not interested in something, we won't be inspired to do much about it. For this reason it's imperative to release yourself from the idea that the list I have just given is somehow more worthwhile than the one that you would draw up yourself. It's true, however, that a third person might insist that my list is more worthwhile if you were to write this:

- Do more baking with the children
- Play more American jazz
- Bit of stonemasonry

But if you were to consider your list from a wider perspective it might be seen to have a grandeur of its own:

- Do more baking with the children = *passing the best of our ancestors to people yet unborn*
- Play more American jazz = *undermine Hitler*
- Bit of stonemasonry = *building a magnificent cathedral for people to worship in long after we've gone*

In other words, if your chosen mission does not immediately appear very ambitious, that may only be because you are admirably modest and haven't yet found the words to express its cosmic significance. If that bothers you, keep asking, 'Why am I doing this?' But fundamentally it's not important, so long as you are pursuing something meaningful to you, and it involves, at some level, helping others.

All the same, it may help to provide a systematic analysis of the kinds of issues facing us. One way to do this is to divide them into four types:

i.   Problems that affect everybody, but for which nobody (or hardly anybody) can imagine a remedy that they, as individuals, can administer. These might include living in a state of war, or under a ruthless dictatorship, or in a lawless environment where violent crime or corruption is widespread.

ii. Problems that appear to affect only some people, and not the population as a whole. For example: the many situations, throughout history, where rights were withheld from certain racial or religious groups, or from women or children; or extremes of poverty that make it almost impossible to live a happy life.

iii. Problems that pose a threat to everybody, but are recognized only by a small minority. This might include issues like climate change, destruction of natural systems, population growth, or resource shortages.

iv. Not problems but opportunities. If the streets around us are ugly, that may bother us a great deal. We may have imagined elegant and efficient ways to run public infrastructure. Or alternative electoral systems. We may have come up with an invention that has the potential to transform people's lives, created beautiful art, or written something insightful.

If the fourth type is on your mind, you are entitled to pursue it without worrying that you should first put an end to war, topple dictators, save the planet, feed the hungry, and cure the sick. The world would be immeasurably poorer, after all, if everybody devoted themselves solely to remedying those great ills, and nobody was available to, for instance, tend gardens any more.

To identify your own greatest concerns, you might try to draw up a shortlist – a top five, perhaps. It may help to ask yourself what you would do if you knew you were certain to succeed – if failure was, magically, impossible. By asking the question that way, we get rid of the nagging internal voice that says we couldn't possibly manage such a thing, and who the hell do we think we are, anyway? So today my own list would read:

i.   Organize a Christmas party for my street.

ii. Find someone to fund a prize for the designer who works out how to extract fibre from nettles cheaply, for use in high-quality sustainable clothing.

iii. Encourage the cooperative movement to launch a parallel currency, creating liquidity for its members at a time when banks are not helping.

iv. Talk to local cafe about providing space for local artists (including children) on its walls.

v.   Set up a webpage enabling local people to upload news.

At all times, strive to be specific. Surprisingly often, people worry about, for instance, 'poverty' or 'animal rights', but have no clear idea what it is about these topics that they want to fix. Nobody can get rid of poverty altogether, because (as Ruskin pointed out) rich and poor are relative terms, like north and south. So what is it about poverty that bothers us? To get to the heart of the matter, we must keep asking ourselves why something is a problem. At first, this seems silly: how can anybody not understand that poverty is a problem? But unless we are specific about what the problem is, we can't hope to find a specific solution.

It's impossible to overstate the importance of this point: if you don't know what you want to fix, it can't be done.

After going through the process carefully, we may discover that our generalized concern about 'poverty' boils down to, say, finding ways for everybody in the world to be clothed and fed. From here, we might decide whether it is clothing or feeding that interests us most. And when we have pinned down exactly what the problem is, we can move on to thinking of ways to help fix it.

Having decided which cause to take up, we must consider the different approaches we might take. Should we stand for election and work to change the law? Join a campaign group? Or 'just' carry out good works quietly by ourselves?

It depends on what it is you are trying to change: each of these approaches is valid, and can produce results, but each also has its downsides. In formal politics, we may achieve a great deal at a stroke, but it could take years before we do this, and we will frequently be required to compromise on the way. We may, for instance, go into politics with one particular mission in mind, and find that our entire career is given over to other things, including policies we don't particularly believe in.

If we act alone, on the other hand, we avoid compromising, but may never feel satisfied that we have achieved enough.

Sometimes, it's perfectly obvious which route needs to be taken. The lawyer and environmentalist Polly Higgins concluded that the best way to stop extensive destruction of ecosystems was to create a new international crime of 'ecocide'.

While it remains legal to engage in destructive practices, she concluded, businesses will continue to do so, if only on the flimsy basis that, if they didn't, somebody else would. And as long as damaging businesses remains legal, they will continue to attract funding and research that would otherwise go towards safer but more expensive projects.

An international law like the one prohibiting genocide would be enforceable against individuals, not companies, and people would be deemed culpable even if they were 'only following orders'. Thus, a law against ecocide would turn subordinates into whistle-blowers: every individual around the world automatically becomes a steward of the environment.

Higgins was inspired by reading about the abolition of the slave trade in Britain in the early 1800s. Campaigners decided it was no use seeking piecemeal improvements in conditions for slaves. They wanted to abolish slavery altogether. In the UK, at the time, 300 companies were engaged in facilitating the slave trade. They fought hard against abolition, arguing that it would lead to a loss of jobs, and that the public wanted slavery to remain in place. They promised better conditions for slaves – fresh hay for bedding was one idea – and said it was best to let the market regulate itself. But slavery was banned, and subsidies for the trade were withdrawn, to be moved to support more benign businesses instead. Within a year, British slave companies were profitably trading in other commodities, including tea and china. 'Corporations and the economy, when faced with the risk of collapse, can reinvent their wheels overnight,' says Higgins, who continues to campaign for change.

To introduce a new law is no small matter. That's not to say it can't happen, but only to warn that a great deal of work must be done first, and by a lot of people, if representatives of nearly 200 countries at the UN are to accept the need for a new law, and enact it.

I talked about this recently with somebody who has devoted herself for decades to formal politics – as a lifelong member of a main-stream party, and a former candidate for the British parliament. I was struck by her determined insistence that the only way to get things changed is to stand for parliament or to vote for people who will enact the 'right' laws. Slavery was abolished, she said, by parliament. Homosexuality was legalized by parliament. Education flourishes because parliament decided that all children must attend school.

I agreed that parliaments made laws in the way she described, but said that the parliamentarians would not have voted for these things if there was not already a strong mandate in the country at large – indeed, they'd have had no right to do so.

The mere enacting of legislation doesn't necessarily make a great deal of difference. Even before the slave trade was abolished, it was entirely possible for people to decide to give up owning slaves, and many who gave the matter some thought did exactly that. What's more, despite the trade having been abolished, slavery continues ille-gally today. Similarly, while homosexuality has been decriminalized in many countries, this does not mean that gay people are freed from

Hope is not a passive thought; it is a call to action.

ordinary, everyday prejudice. And though parliament obliges parents to send their children to school, astonishingly large numbers of children leave school unable to read.

The tenth-century Danish King of England, Canute, was once told by his advisers that he was so powerful he could stop the waves if he wanted to do so. To prove them wrong, he went to the beach and commanded the waves to stop. It would be well if people remembered that parliament's power is no greater than Canute's: merely banning or legalizing something does not *necessarily* make a great difference. The thing that makes a difference is people deciding to comply – and as we've seen, they can change their behaviour without the intervention of parliament.

If you want people to feel that they have the capacity to change things, it's extremely important to draw attention to the ways they can do that *themselves*. If, instead, you insist that they must wait for somebody else to do it on their behalf, you make them feel powerless, and rob them of responsibility, which is necessary and wholesome. Unless we feel that we can do something ourselves, we have no hope, says the writer and activist Rebecca Solnit. 'Hope is not like a lottery ticket you can sit on the sofa and clutch, feeling lucky. Hope is an axe you break down doors with. Hope calls for action.'

Another friend frequently complained about the greed of bankers. I asked him which bank he uses. It was one of the global giants, implicated historically in all kinds of shady behaviour. He would like banks, he said, along with railways and other utilities, to be taken into national ownership. I pointed out that he could have the kind of banking he wants right now if he switched to an account run by a bank that is owned by ordinary people like him, as a cooperative with strict ethical-investment policies. Why wait – perhaps for ever – for parliament to make obligatory what he could have at once? He said he was too lazy to change, and anyway wanted parliament to make ethical banking a matter of policy, so that it would be available to everyone.

I was puzzled that a man who gives up hours to knock on strangers' doors on behalf of a political party could describe himself as 'too lazy', but I assured him it doesn't take long to move bank accounts, and that the facility is *already* available to everyone who cares to take advantage of it. If people don't want it, that's fine. What right does he have to try to impose on others something he can't even be bothered to take advantage of himself?

The best that can be said for parliament is that it enacts legislation as a projection, by no means perfect, of the will of the majority. People who are not happy about the status quo, like my friend, often assume that they need only to get parliament to enact a new law and then their own vision will be imposed on everybody else. But in order to make that happen, it may sometimes feel like we have to wage war on government itself.

People who have tried to make change in the past have often done so spontaneously, and intuitively. How much more effective might they have been, Gene Sharp wondered, if they'd had a better idea of what had been done before? And so he set about compiling a list of methods of non-violent action, which stalled for years at precisely 198. (The term 'non-violent action' is inelegant, and may strike some people as countercultural. But nobody seems to have been able to devise a better way to describe the many everyday methods of creating change that happen not to involve violence.)

The techniques Sharp lists include examples that go back as far as recorded history, and come from all over the world. Number 67, 'flight of workers', can be said to have been used by Moses and the Israelites as a way to register dissatisfaction with the conduct of Pharoah. Number 90, 'revenue refusal', was used in Ancient China by unwilling taxpayers, who buried their possessions and took to the hills when the tax collector was known to be on his way. Number 57, 'Lysistratic non-action', may have been used by women in Ancient Greece to end war by refusing sexual relations with bellicose men, but Sharp has found evidence of the technique being used in recent history by both women of the Iroquois nation and in Southern Rhodesia, as it was then called. It was used in Kenya more recently, by women who included the wife of the president.

Some of the techniques appear almost boringly familiar, such as technique number 2, 'letters of opposition or support'. But they can still be effective, and in certain contexts, even that step requires courage. In her book *Wild Swans,* Jung Chang describes the enormous hardship her family suffered during China's Cultural Revolution, due in large part to her father's decision, as a loyal, high-ranking official, to write a letter of comradely concern to Chairman Mao. And even in supposedly free-thinking countries, it can be dangerous to put in writing opinions that go against the general consensus. You may not be incarcerated, but you may lose your job.

Other techniques require physical bravery, such as technique number 171, 'non-violent interjection', as practised by that anonymous

Chinese man before the tanks at Tiananmen Square. Or technique 66, 'total personal non-cooperation'. During World War II a conscientious objector in the US named Corbett Bishop declined to eat, dress himself or even stand up. His limp body had to be carried in and out of court and a variety of prison cells. He was forcibly fed by tube. Eventually, after considerable newspaper publicity, he was allowed home without agreeing to anything.

Many of the techniques compiled by Sharp usually require the participation of more than one person. Technique 193, 'overloading of administrative systems', was used in the US during the Vietnam War. The law relating to the draft required individuals to give notice within ten days of 'any change in address or status'. The large numbers of people opposed to the war decided to take this so seriously that officials were overwhelmed. People wrote in to state that they had moved to a different room in the same house. Others wrote that they were thinking of travelling, then wrote again to say they had changed their minds. The same technique has been used more recently to crash official computer systems.

Sharp's list of 198 methods of non-violent action is included in the appendix to this book, and rewards further study. As we scrutinize it, we observe a broad distinction between the various techniques.

The first group is gathered by Sharp under the general heading of 'protest', but if that puts you off, think of it as 'raising awareness'.

The second group of techniques is described by Sharp as non-cooperation. You may prefer to think of this as simply ceasing to have dealings with systems or people you dislike – for instance, not buying items made by companies that exploit their workers, or refusing to fly in order to reduce CO_2 emissions.

The third group can be classified as active interventions to disrupt the status quo, perhaps by building alternatives to what is currently available. Again, these innovations need not be especially 'alternative' in the pejorative sense. Nor do they need to pose a threat to the status quo. One fantastically successful example was the Scout movement, founded by the soldier Robert Baden-Powell because he was dismayed by the poor state of recruits sent to fight for Britain in the Boer War. He decided to do something about it, and took a group of young men to camp for a few days on a small island. Despite that modest beginning – and his narrowly pro-British, militaristic motivation – the Scout Movement spread around the world and became utterly mainstream.

As with warfare, it's necessary to have a strategy before you choose your tactics. But the techniques need not always be negative, in the sense of involving withdrawal or hostility. Japanese unions, working for employers who used just-in-time delivery, invented the 'go-faster' strike to support their demand for better pay. I came across a similar example from the UK. A library was threatened with closure owing to budget cuts. Local residents joined forces to withdraw every single book from that library, leaving every shelf bare. (In a witty flourish, they arranged it so that the very last book to be taken out would be Mary Norton's novel, *The Borrowers*.) Which is to say: they opposed the planned closure by showing that they really did use the library.

The tactic is so elegant that it appears obvious, and even unremarkable. But in light of it we can see the ineptness of others who, out of desperation in a similar situation, might have chosen different tactics – throwing paint over the local mayor, for instance, or embarking on a hunger strike.

How do we decide which techniques are required in our own case? We might start by brainstorming, either by ourselves or with help from friends. It doesn't actually matter whether they share our aspiration, only that they are willing, briefly, to pretend they do and to come up with some ideas. They may enjoy the exercise more if they *don't* share your view, as this allows them to think freely. A psychological experiment carried out decades ago found that businessmen taking a creativity test scored very poorly indeed until they were asked to take the test again, 'as if they were hippies', whereupon the same dull individuals put down ideas that were startlingly imaginative. In the same way, if people who don't share your particular concern allow themselves to pretend briefly that they do, they may provide better ideas than a group that is genuinely like-minded.

Whether brainstorming alone or with others, the key thing is to put ideas down on paper. It doesn't matter whether they are earnest or frivolous, practical or impractical. Just put down whatever comes to mind, without censoring, explaining or defending anything. Don't criticize or even praise other people's ideas either, till the process is complete.

When you have collected a large number of ideas – at least twenty – read through them carefully. Remove any that do not seem helpful. After that, take a fresh look and select the ones that seem most helpful. After just five minutes of brainstorming, you may discover ideas that verge on genius.

4. Bearing Witness

Of course not everyone will identify a particular mission of their own. The good news is that this need not stop us having a powerful effect, because we can change the world both by passing on news about things that need fixing, and by helping promote other people's attempts to fix those things.

It's possible that these two types of message appeal to slightly different personality types – pessimists may gravitate towards pointing out problems, while optimists are likely to enjoy talking about and coming up with solutions. But both types of information are important. You may know already, but to find out which appeals to you more – and perhaps more importantly, what *kinds* of problems and solutions you are interested in – pay close attention to the sort of stories you tell people. Do you talk about climate change worsening? Shops closing? People's bad manners? Or are you more likely to enthuse about exciting new inventions and tell people about opportunities to see inspiring events? If this doesn't work, read several newspapers over a single weekend, and write a summary. Which kinds of stories grabbed you? Did you focus more on problems, or solutions? It doesn't matter if writing doesn't come easily. Bearing witness has always been an important part of changing the world.

For Jung Chang, who worshipped Mao as a child in China, the process of enlightenment was gradual. Crucially, she was able to question ideas with others – if only close relatives. In *Wild Swans* she discusses the effect of her younger brother Jin-ming's more sceptical view of the regime:

> Jin-ming often made sceptical comments . . . which kept us laughing. This was unusual in those days, when humour was dangerous. Mao, hypocritically calling for 'rebellion', wanted no genuine inquiry or scepticism. To be able to think in a sceptical way was my first step towards enlightenment. Jin-ming helped to destroy my rigid habits of thinking.

The importance of these voices – educated, questioning and critical – cannot be underestimated. Jung Chang's mind, and those of countless Chinese citizens around her, were changed not by laws or initiatives or rebellions, but by the commentary that they heard all around them.

When Mao's efficient deputy Zhou Enlai died, Mao's wife and her political faction known as the Gang of Four ordered that mourning for Zhou be played down. But many people ignored the order, and showed grief in order to express disapproval of the Gang. Soon afterwards other, small acts of protest were seen across China: at the endless mass meetings, speakers read their prepared scripts in flat, expressionless voices, and their audiences wandered around chatting, knitted or even went to sleep. As acts of subversion, these seem unremarkable but the cumulative effect was decisive – after Mao died, his wife and the Gang of Four were quickly and easily arrested.

If we decide to take a more direct approach to spreading awareness and enlightenment, we should proceed with caution. Remember that there is only one way to get anybody to do anything: by making them *want* to do it. And that applies even to changing their minds.

Don't begin by discussing things on which you differ, advised Dale Carnegie in his bestselling self-improvement manual *How To Win Friends and Influence People*. Begin by emphasizing areas of agreement. The idea is to keep the other person saying yes, yes, and at all costs to stop them saying no, because once they've said no, they may feel that to change their mind would be to lose face. You are more likely to get them to say yes if you have attempted to understand their interests. Try sincerely to see things from the other person's point of view, Carnegie adds. Don't just pretend, because if it's not sincere, it's useless.

This is how salesmen work. It's also how the Ancient Greek philosopher Socrates worked. He asked people questions to which the answer was likely to be affirmative, and kept doing it until they had moved, often without realizing it, into accepting a position they would have rejected only moments before. To give an example from my own experience: the man who owned the flat I used to share with friends wanted to increase our rent at the end of the year. We could not afford to pay the increase. I called him to say we would have to leave, with regret, but asked if he had been happy with us as tenants. Yes, he said. I said that I expected he might have to pay a fee to an agency to find new tenants. Yes, he said glumly. I asked if he would lose money if the flat were empty for a short period. Yes, he said, he would. I pointed out that the increased income he hoped for by rais-ing the rent would be lost if the flat stayed empty for as little as two weeks. Did he think that was a possibility? It was, he said. I added that even after paying the agent's fee, he might end up with tenants he didn't get on with. Might it not, on reflection, be better all round if he kept the rent at the level we could afford? He agreed to do so, and we stayed another year.

This kind of open conversation will not always work out the way we want it to but it's infinitely better than strident confrontation, which can be irritating and cause distress. It could even be worse than that: lecturing people about, for example, environmental collapse without at the same time giving them a sense of agency could make them depressed and even ill because, as Frankl saw, people need a sense of purpose if they are to cope with adversity. Research suggests that this partly explains high sickness levels among the long-term unemployed.

To paraphrase the late philosopher Raymond Williams, the key thing is not to make despair convincing but to make hope possible.

This is what Trenna Cormack has tried to do. Instead of being a prophet of doom, she became a prophet of hope. A few years ago, at a party, a young woman (Cormack) came up to me and asked if I might be interested in looking at a book she had written and published herself. Out of mere politeness, I said I would. And when I did so, I was very impressed. Cormack had been in the paying audience at an event some time earlier called 'Be the Change' – a phrase borrowed from Gandhi, who conjured us to 'Be the change you want to see in the world'. The topics covered by the speakers at the event included many that are often presented in dismal terms, including environmental crisis and social injustice, but Cormack was startled to find the discourse was generally upbeat. 'I found myself in a hall full of people who cared passionately about creating a better world,' she said. Over three days, they heard from many speakers engaged in a variety of inspiring activities. 'I thought to myself, "This is brilliant! There should be a book about this."'

And then the question was turned to the audience: 'This isn't just about sages on stages. What are you going to do to *be* the change you wish to see? What's yours to do?' Cormack gulped and realized that the book she had imagined was to be her own work. She made arrangements, interviewed dozens of people who inspired her, wrote them up, published the book herself, and went out to promote it herself too.

She did not set out to highlight any particular cause of her own, but through her efforts she helped others' causes to be better known.

A Canadian art dealer named Fred Mulder did much the same to spread awareness of people actively working to overturn intractable problems. Mulder used to give money to good causes but without feeling entirely satisfied. Then he got together with a handful of others and set up The Funding Network as a forum for philanthropists (even modest philanthropists, with only small heaps of cash to disburse) to learn together about social-change projects and help fund them as a group. Representatives of interesting and worthy causes are invited to 'pitch' to TFN audiences of would-be funders at regular networking events. In less than a decade, thousands of sponsors have raised millions of pounds for hundreds of good causes, and spin-off networks have been established internationally.

But it's not necessary to go to the same lengths as Cormack and Mulder. Even just the odd word here and there can be helpful. A friend of mine had, on a few rare occasions, spoken to me of the help he had found at Alcoholics Anonymous, an organization of which I then knew little; but those few words enabled me, when the dire need arose, to recommend AA to another close friend, who was thereby utterly transformed.

5. What You Will Need

By now you should have discovered what sort of cause you want to help with, and your place within it. So we are almost ready to start our adventure, but one last thing remains necessary. We must consider the resources we may need, and the allies.

Physical resources may be important, but what I have in mind at this point are personal qualities: skills, experience, mental and emotional capacities. Things that you might list on a job application – but also some that you probably wouldn't.

To get a better grasp of my own skills, I recently drew up a list of my work experience, including some things I had done only as a pastime, holiday job, or tiresome duty. I resolved from now on to stop thinking of myself only as a writer. I am also an artist, a baker, a career coach, a carpenter, a cleaner, a cook, a copywriter, a decorator, a dog walker, an English-language teacher, a film-maker, a gardener, a map-maker, a bike messenger, a minicab driver, a poet, a police-checked child minder, a qualified first-aider, a printer, a publisher, a rubbish collector, a Scout patrol leader, a second-hand bookseller, a tailor, a typist, a waiter, a washer-up and possibly much else. I have to say that drawing up this list gave quite a boost to my self-esteem.

We can all draw up a list of work experience, skills and hobbies, but we rarely look for potential in our limits and our shortcomings.

We might be surprised to find something valuable there. This sounds like another paradox, but it's not.

Take Richard Reynolds. He lives in a tower block in a part of London with few green spaces. A few years ago he started to clean up the municipal planter on the vast roundabout near his home, removing all the cigarette ends people had discarded. Then he began to put in some plants. Over time, he learned which plants did well, and which didn't. Sometimes vandals destroyed plants. At other times local officials interfered, telling him he had no right to do what he was doing. But other local people were inspired, and joined him. Gradually they moved on to other spaces, including a large traffic island, which they planted with rows of lavender. Over time, word got out about Reynolds' work, and he heard from others doing similar things elsewhere. They set up a movement of 'guerilla gardeners', which has since gone mainstream. Not long ago I walked past one of London's big department stores and saw Reynolds' face on materials in its window display. The store was selling 'guerilla gardening kits'. The seeds he had planted were flourishing, in more ways than one.

The point to remember is that Reynolds' success stems from a very peculiar blessing: he has no garden of his own.

To see the potential even in our shortcomings, failures, and what we lack requires us to take a fresh look at our entire lives. If we are to recognize their value, it's not our resources that must change: it's the way we see them. This means seizing any opportunity to transfigure them, rather than overlooking, or shunning them. It's about being creative, and looking on the bright side – not coming up with reasons to be cheerful that are far-fetched and implausible but finding genuine value and potential. In all likelihood, we will find strengths even – perhaps especially – in areas that we don't much like to think about.

It is often argued that the strongest among us are those who have been through the greatest difficulties. (As Nietzsche put it, what doesn't kill us makes us stronger.) The charity Peace Direct offers financial support and advice to community-based peacemakers all around the world. Many of the individuals carrying out the work are former child soldiers, who have done shameful things. Ordinarily, that background would be viewed as a shortcoming, but in the circumstances it makes these individuals well-qualified to help others seek peace.

In other words, what we need is often exactly what we already have.

A less sensational way to look at this might be to consider whether, say, the work that you find boring may after all be the means by which you can achieve wonderful things. In the ancient Buddhist 'Song of Zazen', Hakuin Zenji wrote: 'How sad that people ignore the near and search afar, like someone in the midst of water crying out with thirst'. This nearly describes something that happened during the Cold War. Russia and the US were racing to get into space, and an American named Paul Fisher took it on himself to spend a vast fortune developing a pen that would write in outer space. NASA duly bought his pens and distributed them to astronauts. The Russians, meanwhile, made do with an alternative so modest that NASA somehow overlooked it – a pencil.

Having considered our resources, we should then take a similarly forensic approach to assessing our allies, because as we have seen, it's unlikely that we will achieve a great deal working entirely alone.

Chris Johnstone, in his work with addicts and alcoholics, encourages them to draw maps of their support network. We might usefully do the same. To begin, write your name in the middle of a piece of paper, and around it write the names of the people who give you the greatest support. Then draw an arrow from each one towards your own name, varying the thickness of the arrow to indicate the amount of support they give (a thick arrow means a lot of support). Now map the support you give to other people by drawing arrows in the opposite direction. Add more names, if necessary.

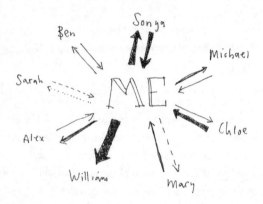

After drawing such a map, you might consider whether there are changes you would like to make – relationships to strengthen, or others to back away from. In the example I've provided, you see that I am giving lots of support to William, but getting nothing back, while Chloe is giving me a great deal of support, and getting little in return. Johnstone suggests that the most promising relationships may not be the ones where the support is strongest but where it is mutual. 'They are valuable resources in your life,' he says. 'Treasure them. Mutual-support arrangements are stronger than one-way flows.'

Now that you have mapped your network, go and tell people what you plan to do and ask for help explicitly, says Johnstone, because when you do this, you liberate helpers to do more than merely nod supportively when you come to them. They start coming to you with ideas. They may even make your project their own.

Instinctively, we find it difficult to ask for help like this. We think it might be an imposition. But there's plenty of evidence that people like being asked: it's flattering. The only reason people might not like being asked is if they can't see a way to say no. So when you ask for help in your mission, make it clear that you don't mind if your people tell you they prefer not to help, for whatever reason – either now or at any time in the future.

If they know they are free to excuse themselves, they will almost never feel the need to exercise that freedom – and together you can do great things.

6. Taking a First Step

Having considered what drives us, and examined carefully the things that need doing, the techniques we might use, and the resources and allies we need, we should be ready to start. But when we think about issues that are huge in scale, we can be overwhelmed. From our first school physics lessons we've grown up with the idea that to move a massive object requires huge force. This is true, but newer insights from physics show that this force can just as easily be derived from a number of smaller movements.

Chaos theory teaches that seemingly insignificant initial circumstances can effect global, even universal events. As the theory has it: a butterfly flaps its wings in one country and helps to cause a tornado in another. The same idea applies in our lives. In her workshops, the environmental activist Joanna Macy uses the following exercise to dramatize something like the 'butterfly effect' in human terms.

She explains the exercise in her book, co-authored with Molly Young Brown, *Coming Back To Life*. It works best with a large group of people, in a large open space. Macy gives instructions: select two other people in the group, without indicating who they may be, and move so as to keep an equal distance between yourself and those two people at all times (not necessarily at the midpoint between them).

People immediately begin to circulate, and each movement triggers many others in an active, interdependent fashion.

> Participants find they are by necessity maintaining wide-angle vision and constant alacrity of response. The process is purposeful, suspenseful, laced with laughter. It speeds up for a while, then may abate, accelerate, and again slow down toward equilibrium, but it rarely comes to stasis.

This continues for four or five minutes, then as activity lessens Macy invites people to pause and reflect on what they experienced. Often participants mention a temporary eclipse of self-consciousness, as perceptions focused not on their own actions so much as on other people's. They've become aware that they are part of something bigger than themselves.

Sometimes, Macy (who joins in the exercise herself) waits for a while before deliberately upsetting the system's balance. Interestingly, people rarely notice who started such a chain of events, but afterwards remember the sudden flurry of activity – and how small, intentional change by just one person can create wide effects.

So: somebody has to go first, or that intentional change won't happen. But why should it be us? One reason we hold back from doing what needs to be done is that nobody *else* seems bothered about it. This comes down to something fundamental about human beings: we're social animals and we learn the right way to behave by observing others.

And yet every single breakthrough occurred because somebody decided to do something new. That first person's actions 'gave permission' to others – if only to do what they already wanted to do.

Not long ago, my colleague at the School of Life, Dr Nick South-gate, told me about a video on the internet, apparently recorded on somebody's phone, featuring a crowd of people in a field at a music festival in Canada (www.youtube.com/watch?v=GA8z7f7a2Pk). In the film, a solitary figure dances in an open space, without the slightest hint of self-consciousness, and continues to do so for some time. A few people walk past but studiously ignore him. Eventually another man joins in. This second man puts energy into his move-ments but appears self-conscious, occasionally looking back into the crowd with a grin, for reassurance. The first man welcomes him, but carries on as before. Then a third man arrives, seemingly a friend of the second one, and makes moves that are obviously intended, more than anything else, to be amusing.

Then three more young men arrive together, and three more dash behind them. People near the camera whoop approval. Six more arrive. And then comes the tipping point: everybody rushes to join in, suddenly desperate not to be left out.

What held them back? Maybe they were too busy filming the dancing man on their cameras: it's sometimes easier to be a specta-tor. There are certainly an awful lot of versions of the event avail-able to watch on the internet. One is particularly instructive: for five minutes, the person holding the camera and his neighbours make horrible remarks about the dancer. But as more people join in, their tone changes. 'Wow, it's a revolution, man!' says a male voice. 'One man can change the world!' says a woman. And after six and a half minutes of filming, she says, 'I wanna go down [and join in]!'

What Dr Southgate told me about the dancing man is instructive for anybody hoping to make change:

> This is an interesting example of what it means to go first. If this one guy doesn't start dancing, the dance will not happen. He does this at lots of festivals. It's his thing. Most times, he dances and no one else dances (or only a few, and it dies out). He knows he has to get up and dance alone for a long time before anything happens. And sometimes he will fail, but if he gets up and does it again, eventually the time and the place and the people will be right and his dance will be seen and his call will be heard.

You might not have thought it was so hard to get people who had chosen to attend a music festival to dance. But the point to emphasize is this: don't worry about other people. If you put enough energy into your own efforts, soon enough they may find it impossible not to join you. Or as Gandhi famously put it: 'Be the change you want to see in the world'.

What the dancing man showed was that we *can* change the ethos of the group around us. Chris Johnstone, in his work with addicts, found that if they were to overcome a climate of cynicism and put-downs, it helped to stop thinking about what other people 'should' do and concentrate instead on what they themselves *will* do. His insight applies to us all, and the social environments we find ourselves in, whether at work or at home or in public life. The key is to recognize the way we ourselves participate in each context. By simply refus-ing to undermine anyone around you, and instead giving positive encouragement to others, you change the culture you live in. And as Johnstone says, 'styles of interaction are contagious'.

It may help to give a more obviously historic example. In the southern states of America, as recently as the 1950s, black people were second-class citizens. Among many other indignities, they could not attend the same schools as white Americans, use the same public toilets, drink from the same water fountains, or sit and eat in shops frequented by white people. Many believed that to complain about this petty humiliation would only result in trouble.

But one day in 1955, four African-American passengers on a bus in Montgomery, Alabama, were asked, as usual, to give up their seats to newly boarded white passengers, and stand. Three complied, but Rosa Parks, a seamstress, refused. At a stroke, she threw off what Gandhi called mental slavery, and substantially inspired the civil-rights movement that followed. But it's important to understand that, just by going first and providing inspiration, she did not become the 'leader'. Going first does not necessarily mean taking charge of everything that follows.

A few days after her arrest, a group called the Women's Political Council called for a one-day bus boycott:

> This has to be stopped. Negroes have rights too, for if Negroes did not ride the buses they could not operate. Three fourths of the riders are Negroes, yet we are arrested, or have to stand over empty seats. If we do not do something to stop these arrests, they will continue. The next time, it may be you, or your daughter, or mother.

Virtually everybody complied, and it was decided to continue with the protest. The original ambition was only to modify slightly the system of segregation, so that black people would not be obliged to stand if there were empty seats available. But the success of the one-day boycott increased people's confidence, and led to calls for wider reforms.

In the months that followed, black people stopped using the buses altogether. They took taxis, walked, or shared cars – a sizeable car pool was organized, largely through church groups.

The protest led to reprisals. The use of taxi journeys at reduced fares was prohibited. Negro drivers, including one prominent protester, Martin Luther King, were arrested for minor, often imaginary driving offences. A hundred prominent protesters were arrested and charged with violating an anti-boycott law. Insurance policies on cars in the car pool were cancelled.

Then victory came. The US supreme court, acting on a suit filed by the protesters, declared segregation on buses to be illegal, not only in Nashville but across the US. But protesters decided to continue to avoid the buses until the ruling came into force, and segregation actually ended. Raising the stakes, the Ku Klux Klan rode through the Negro district. But this didn't have the usual effect. Instead of finding the inhabitants terrified, locked away in houses with the lights off, the Klan found people were sitting on doorsteps to watch. Some even waved.

On the first day the buses were officially integrated, there were no problems. But then white extremists began a reign of terror, with beatings and shootings. Churches and homes were bombed. The Klan paraded again and burned crosses. But the protesters

I shall not be moved: Rosa Parks started the bus boycott, and wider civil rights campaigns, by refusing to give up her seat to a white passenger.

kept their discipline. Many in the white community were repelled by the violence that was supposedly being enacted on their behalf, including the local newspaper, church ministers and a local business association. The terrorism abruptly ceased. Segregation on buses, in Montgomery and everywhere else, had ended, and pretty well everybody accepted a state of affairs that would have seemed unthinkable less than a year before.

Soon after, as a result of the wider struggle, black people were granted equality in other areas too.

But that may seem to suggest a kind of historical inevitability. Civil rights for black people were not inevitable. Rosa Parks is a celebrated symbol of the struggle, but she didn't pull it off on her own. A vast number of other people, perhaps inspired by her example, took personal responsibility and refused to submit any longer.

It would be a mistake to presume that these individuals were exceptional, or indeed that they acted without fear. They felt the fear and did it anyway. Diane Nash was only twenty-one years old, in 1959, when she coordinated sit-ins at lunch counters in Nashville reserved for white people. Like others involved, Nash had been trained beforehand in how to conduct herself, at a workshop on non-violence. But she was surrounded by an angry, shouting mob and for a period of fifteen minutes she wobbled: 'I gave myself a short period to make a decision. Either I would resign as chairperson because I could not be effective, or I would overcome the fear and get my mind back on my work,' she recalls, in Catherine Ingram's *In The Footsteps of Gandhi*.

In the event, Nash managed to calm herself, and stayed. In the years since, she has been upset by the way historians and the media focus on a few prominent leaders, such as Parks, or Martin Luther King:

> Martin was not the leader. He was the spokesman, a very competent, eloquent spokesman. He was a great man. But if people think of him as superhuman or a saint, then when something needs to be changed they are tempted to say, 'I wish we had a leader like Martin Luther King today.' People need to know that it was just people like themselves who thought up the strategies and managed the movement. Charismatic leadership has not freed us and it never will, because freedom is, by definition, people realizing that they are their own leaders.

III. What Needs Changing, and How

1. Add Beauty – and Fun

Bringing about positive change often takes the form of reducing suffering. But many of us, while recognizing war, poverty and environmental collapse as grave problems, just don't feel inclined, or qualified, to fix them.

We may feel that there's something a bit dutiful, grey and depressing about attempting to save the world from famine, or eliminating disease. (Quite apart from it being hard work.) We recognize that the task might appeal to *someone*, but it doesn't appeal to us. In fact, the prospect of getting involved in something like that may make us glum, or leave us bored. And recognizing that is important, because feeling bored is a sure sign that we have not found the kind of meaningful activity that makes life not just endurable but actually enjoyable.

But there are two ways to change the world: to decrease suffering or increase pleasure.

And we may instinctively prefer the latter. Like many others, we may be drawn to the aesthetic side of life. If this sounds rarefied, that's not intended. It's not about knuckling down to study art history (which some people might find just as boring as tackling famine). Nor is it even, necessarily, about the so-called fine arts. We may want to paint or make sculpture, certainly, but many would prefer to learn a few guitar chords and start a band. Or we may be drawn to traditional handicrafts, in the widest sense: not just embroidery or jewellery-making but also customizing second-hand clothes, doing DIY or inventing amazing things in a secret workshop. Taking an even wider look at creative engagement, we may dream of opening a small cafe or running a hotel.

These wishes may seem initially entirely selfish. But we needn't beat ourselves up about this, because when we engage creatively with the world, we are having an impact. Our work can lighten hearts, console, and give people a reason to think of life as something to savour rather than just endure. Works of art (in this widest sense) are ways of building a meaningful community, tools of communication – and thus not unconnected to the more overtly 'serious' mission of peacekeepers and global diplomats.

History shows that as soon as people's most basic needs are taken care of, the aesthetic impulse kicks in. We want to write stories, sing of our pain (or make people laugh), and create works of harmonious and delicate craftsmanship. These needs are at the heart of what we are, and should never be sacrificed to a misplaced notion of serious-ness – or put away for ever just because a teacher, years ago, said something unkind about our early efforts.

All too often, we think of art as a luxury, or something that should be left to 'artists', but the distinction between artists and the rest of us is false. (Was Van Gogh an artist? During his lifetime, nobody wanted to buy his paintings.) Everybody belongs somewhere on a spectrum of creativity, from Mozart performing his most complex works to a toddler taking a first piano lesson. We may think that solving world poverty is the more important pursuit, but changing the world is also about considering our own interests and skills – we will be most effective if we do what comes naturally to us.

Taking part in the aesthetic side of life doesn't mean trying to be famous or make a career of it. Most of us won't make our fortune from art, but we all have the chance, indeed usually the need, to create something beautiful. And if we find that enjoyable, we may find ourselves irresistibly compelled to share it.

Rachael Matthews is an artist and a 'Brother' in London's ancient Art Workers' Guild (there are no 'Sisters'). In her own art, Matthews happens to work with textiles, particularly knitting and crochet. She feels strongly that the satisfaction she derives from her work comes not merely from the finished product but the process involved in making it. And that too is something she wants to share with others. In order to do so, she and her friends sometimes conduct 'knit-ins' on the London Underground. They teach strangers to knit or crochet and let them take away wool and needles if they enjoy it.

A wider-ranging attempt to share the joys of creativity is *Learning To Love You More*, which was devised by the artists Miranda July and Harrell Fletcher. In their own work, Fletcher and July have to come up with original ideas every day, but they realized over years of practice that some of their most joyful and even profound experiences arose through following somebody else's instructions. By letting go of the need to be original, and by following another's idea, they were able to create works of delightful originality.

In order to share something like that sense of liberation – to help others do away with the oppressive instinct for originality – Fletcher and July hit on the charming idea of getting the general

Assignment 63: Make an encouraging banner. (This is one by Sarah Corbett of the Craftivist Collective.)

public to do a number of quasi-artistic and psychological assignments, and then to post their results on a website (www.learning toloveyoumore.com).

There were seventy assignments in all. They included: 'Draw the news', 'Make an encouraging banner', 'Start a lecture series', 'Give advice to yourself in the past', 'Spend time with a dying person', 'Perform the phone call somebody else wished they could have', 'Photograph strangers holding hands' . . .

Some of the other assignments were more introspective, but all shared the quality of inviting people to engage directly with their community and the wider world. In the course of carrying out the assignments, the thousands of people who uploaded reports needed to overcome fear (think of what it takes to ask two people who don't know each other to hold hands!) and to use their creativity. Having done that, they became just as 'expert' as Fletcher and July. One American family successfully completed every assignment and was invited to put on a show at a local gallery. The family's lecture series took the theme 'Art Is Where You Find it, and Everyone Can Do Art'.

I mention this project because it seems typical of what the best works of art can do: reconnect us to sources of energy and engagement that can be stifled by routine and habit.

A good world is not a world where everybody fixates on global problems according to some externally imposed framework of 'importance'. A good world is one in which people find meaning in the particular things they do – and that means a world that has a place for beauty, creativity and play.

2. How Does Money Fit In?

Of all the things that hold us back, our thoughts about money are perhaps the most confusing. And one reason for this is that it can feel as if we face a choice between doing good and making a decent living – we think that we can't choose both.

For most people, this dilemma appears only some time after we embark on our career. We may have started out with excitement in a job that offered glamour or financial rewards, but gradually found it unsatisfying, and have come to envy people whose work seems more meaningful. Alternatively, we may have taken the path of meaningful good works, and have come to resent our low wages and lack of other benefits.

Either way, if this worries us we must work to fix the situation, perhaps change our career. But is it really necessary to make a choice between making a useful contribution and earning a decent living? I don't believe it is. And I'm not going to suggest that the way round the problem is to change the world in our spare time, in evenings and at weekends. (Though we can do that too.) I'm going to insist that we can do good even when we are at work – and we must. Because as we saw in this book's first chapter, we make a difference all the time, and that necessarily includes the time we are at work.

If we are lucky, we may find a way to make a living – perhaps an extremely comfortable living – precisely by doing good. One who has managed that is Dale Vince, a former hippy who made it his mission to generate 'clean' electricity and reduce carbon emissions (because he felt he could not wait for the British government, or anybody else, to do this). He built his own wind turbine, then another, and many more, and set up a company, Ecotricity, to sell his 'green' energy to households and businesses. In the process, he made a fortune.

Making a fortune was not Vince's specific aim, but he has always insisted that his business should succeed *as a business*, for the reason – obvious but worth stating clearly – that otherwise it will fail. (People who consider themselves 'progressive', and instinctively distrust 'business', may want to reflect on this.) And many others have done something similar, finding a mechanism to make meaningful change that generates income, and creates jobs.

But not everybody is naturally inclined to be an entrepreneur. And only a relatively small number can find employment with the likes of Vince. What about the rest? What if the only local employer is rather less admirable?

One way to change how we think about this is to consider honestly how we make our living. Are we serving people's real needs, like Vince, or artificial and unhelpful desires?

Anyone who has raised children will know that it's sometimes necessary to step between them and the things they wish for – such as late bedtime and sugary treats. Sadly, that tendency to behave or consume in ways that are unhelpful is not something we grow out of, and great fortunes have been made by selling things that people do not really need, and may cause harm.

We could all draw up our own list of what those nasty things are. I'm not here to impose my own list on you, but many people would agree that weapons, unhealthy foods and pornography are among them. Nevertheless, the people involved in making and selling these things would usually argue (if you could get them onto the subject, which I suspect they would try to avoid) that they are serving a legitimate need. They might argue that their weapons are needed to keep the peace, their food is a great convenience to people who lack time to make healthy meals from scratch, and their pornography consoles people who are lonely. Are they deluding themselves? Perhaps. But that's not what concerns me here. What I want to propose is that there is no absolutely categorical way to distinguish between 'good' and 'bad' ways to make a living.

This may puzzle some people. Surely I can see that somebody working in an investment bank has sold their soul to the devil? And that somebody who works for an NGO in developing countries is a saint? And haven't I just held up Dale Vince as a paragon?

In reality, it is not so simple. Having met Vince and talked to him for a long time, I do believe that he has built his company, Ecotricity, out of the best intentions, rather than merely a selfish determination to get rich (he pays himself a small salary, less than some colleagues, and has a modest home). But many other people, even if they acknowledge Vince's good intentions, say that wind energy may not be the solution to the energy crisis. They raise arguments against his approach that cannot be dismissed out of hand. Such is the complexity of the relationships between intentions and outcomes that I've discovered it often becomes rather meaningless to attach the labels 'good' and 'bad' to individuals, and perhaps even more so to do that with companies, and entire industry sectors.

Let's consider, as I have already mentioned them, banks and NGOs. I met a man recently who runs the British branch of a Dutch bank that has uncommonly high ethical standards (regarding the kinds of investments they will make), and sometimes lends to good causes that can't provide the customary forms of security. (The loan is made on what essentially amounts to trust, and personal relationships.) On both counts, Charles Middleton and his investment bank, Triodos, deserve applause. I have also met people who told me of NGO activities in developing countries that are downright unhelpful. To give just one quick example: well-known and respected NGOs in developing countries frequently offer a dollar to anybody who attends their events. This enables them to report back to global headquarters that they are winning large audiences – success! But in the process it skews the local economy, because it can be more lucrative to attend a talk than to work, and it puts people off attending other, non-paying events, which may be very important.

But to say that no job or industry is *necessarily* good or bad is not to say that anything goes. It's to insist on personal responsibility. Whether we work in an investment bank or an NGO, the things we do as individuals are either helpful or unhelpful. Speaking for myself, I suspect that I would not find a way to be happy working with weapons, unhealthy food or pornography, and would try hard to find other work elsewhere, but I accept that there may be people working in those areas trying to make real improvements – perhaps by changing the direction of the company, or industry, from within.

Whatever our own position, it's always tempting to be judgemental about other people. To give a perhaps far-fetched example, a highly professional assassin might sneer at a hopelessly un-businesslike charity worker, and vice versa. It's also tempting to justify ourselves ('I only assassinate bad guys' or 'I haven't time to be businesslike').

But we must resist these temptations and look carefully and honestly at what we ourselves actually do, to judge whether we have what Buddhists call a 'right livelihood'.

The way we support ourselves can either allow us to live by our real values or it can distort them. If we decide that our living is unwholesome, we must find another. But the Buddhist idea of right livelihood extends beyond our own job, because we can't be living by our real values while we depend on others to carry out jobs that distort those same values. A teacher may congratulate herself for nurturing children, for example, but would breach her own values if she bought products from companies that use child labour.

In other words, right livelihood is not just a personal matter, but a form of collective responsibility. We are partly responsible for the way others support themselves, because in our daily lives we buy products and services from them or support them through our taxes.

If we hear about companies that breach our values, and if we care about that, it is not enough just to blame others. We should ask what we are doing ourselves to remedy the situation. We should resolve to help create a society where there is more right livelihood and less wrong livelihood, says the Buddhist philosopher Thich Nhat Hanh.

But he adds that nobody, in the real world, can have entirely right livelihood. Once we recognize that, we acquire the humility to stop judging others and ourselves – and get on with our good work.

Another way money can trouble us is related to the idea of giving it away. This is a proven mechanism for making change, but it's often done without the careful attention it deserves.

Specifically, there are three things to consider: how much we can afford to give, whether our donations are truly effective, and whether we should tell others about our donations or remain silent.

Toby Ord has investigated these points thoroughly, not only in his work as a tenured academic philosopher, but in his private life. He has made calculations, and drawn up arguments, that can help us all to understand the distribution of money better.

When Ord was an undergraduate, he often used to make idealistic statements about politics. 'And people would say "Well, if that's what you think, why don't you give all your money to Africa?"' This usually shut him up, he told me, but over time he thought about it. 'If we care about suffering and we want to help people then how much can we achieve?'

He was also directly inspired by something Peter Singer had written, which might make anybody sit up: 'Are you opposed to the present division of resources between the wealthy nations and the poor ones? If you are, and you live in one of the wealthy nations, what are you doing about it? How much of your own surplus income are you giving to one of the many organisations that are helping the poorest of the poor?'

As an academic, Ord does not enjoy massive wealth, but on the other hand he is not badly off. This is how many people would describe their situation. But exactly how well off are we? Ord has set up a movement, Giving What We Can, and a website (www.givingwhatwecan.org) that allows visitors to do the same sums he did himself. Simply type in your annual income (after tax) and the number of people in your household, and the site will generate a report showing how much you can realistically afford to give.

In Ord's own case, the calculations showed that he was among the richest 4 per cent of people in the world, *even taking account of how much further money goes in developing countries*; and that if he gave away 10 per cent of his income, he would still be among the richest 5 per cent.

'Most people are very surprised to find out how rich they really are because we typically compare our wealth only with that of our peers,' Ord said in an interview with me. 'We may or may not be richer than our friends or colleagues, but we are nevertheless richer than the great majority of the world's population. Did we *earn* this position? No. It is certainly true that we can increase our incomes with hard work, but the biggest factor is simply that we were born in the right place – something we can take no credit for at all.'

On his website, Ord has incorporated a graph showing just how unevenly income is distributed. The graph isn't entirely accurate, because to take the super-rich into account it would reach a kilometre above your computer screen.

The more he learned, the more Ord was determined to give money. He felt inspired to set up Giving What We Can, and others joined him – pledging to give away at least 10 per cent of their income – forever.

We may not feel ready to go so far. But if we are resolved to give money, we come to the second problem: how can we be sure that our donations will be effective?

For Ord, the answer came after he happened to read a friend's medical textbook, which compared the efficacy of various medical interventions, and their cost. He was astounded to find that some interventions are 10,000 times more effective than others, but carry the same price. 'Imagine how you would feel if you went into the high street and found one shop selling the same thing as the shop next door for 10,000 times as much!' Of course that wouldn't happen, because the market wouldn't allow it. 'But with charities it does. Two people could each give £1,000 to two charities and one would save a single person's life for a year and the other might save many people a total of 10,000 years of life. And they wouldn't know!'

Ord realized that, by supporting the most cost-effective interventions, he could personally secure 400,000 years of good-quality life for people less privileged than himself. Four hundred thousand? 'That's a lot of life!'

According to the medical textbook, those most cost-effective interventions can buy somebody a whole year of good health for about the price of a decent loaf of bread – by tackling neglected tropical diseases that cause blindness, kidney damage and disfigurement.

It's not very glamorous, but glamour wasn't Ord's motivation. By choosing something this cost-effective, he found he could save a life *every day*. 'You might think that to achieve these amazing things you have to give up your career and move to another country to work for an NGO. But you don't have to do that. You can carry on with whatever career you like.'

When Ord told me this, I was impressed, and glad that I didn't need to give up my work. But also confused. These neglected diseases may have been the most sensible use of my money, but I didn't feel drawn to them. They weren't for me. Anyway, if everybody tackled these tropical diseases they would no longer be neglected, which would be great, but every other cause would suffer. Is it bad to give money, sometimes, to people who shake collecting tins outside train stations for causes we haven't investigated thoroughly?

Ord does not propose that everybody should give money to the same causes as him. But he does suggest that we think carefully about the money we give away – just as we would think carefully before giving somebody a birthday present. It isn't the amount of money we spend that determines a good result, it's the amount of time we're willing to think about what the recipient actually needs – what they're like and what might benefit them individually. Good philanthropy is no different from good birthday-present buying. To help those who wish to donate to causes other than the fight against tropical disease, Ord is working on providing models of cost-efficiency relating to a variety of other interventions in health, education, sanitation and political change.

Another source of advice on giving money effectively is the Institute for Philanthropy. This was set up to advise people with large sums to disburse, but offers insights that would help anybody. Indeed, a key point made on its courses and in its literature is that philanthropy does not always come down to giving money – we can also share our time and expertise. But giving money is important, and the institute was set up precisely to promote that practice by raising awareness of others who do it – because, as we've seen, one of the things that may hold us back when it comes to making any kind of change is the feeling that others are not doing it – and we don't want to feel like suckers.

This raises a crucial question: if we give money, should we speak openly about it, or keep it secret?

Most religious traditions entreat us to avoid making a show of giving alms. 'Do not sound a trumpet before thee, as the hypocrites do,' Jesus said, 'that they may have glory of men.' Making our gift secret preserves the identity of the recipient, notes the Koran.

We should bear these points in mind before giving money in return for, say, a glittering plaque on the wall commemorating our generosity. But giving money publicly does not need to be showy, and nor does it need to humiliate the recipients. 'Public giving can be annoying,' Ord concedes. 'But there is a middle way – doing it without being boastful.'

And the key to not being boastful is to remember that all of us stand in need of charity. It might not be you right now, and you may never contract a tropical disease, but none of us get through life without occasionally relying on the help of others, help that we can't just buy. It's useful to bear this in mind, if you are prone to embarrassment about giving. You may be giving now, but one day you will be at the receiving end – and so have no reason to feel either proud or self-conscious.

If we care about a cause enough to give our own money to it, we would presumably like others to do the same. We can help that to happen by speaking out about the cause itself, and mentioning, modestly, that we have given it our own support. The idea is not to corner people into an awkward position where they feel obliged to follow suit, but only to give them a kind of 'permission' – to stop *them* feeling that they are doing something strange or boastful.

3. Make It Appealing

When we talk about the solving of 'problems' we may put people's backs up or bore them, because most of us naturally associate problems with what is grim and unpleasant. Indeed, if we present only the negative aspects of what the future holds, people will switch off altogether. To change that, we must learn to seduce our audiences into seeing the upsides of a challenge – and one of the best ways to do this is to build networks of friendship around problems.

The environmental movement has been particularly guilty of making us despondent, with seemingly endless tales of doom. And as we've seen, to put people in a place of despondency – to draw attention to danger without also giving a sense of agency – does nothing but render them lethargic, rebellious or depressed. It can actually make people ill, as Frankl observed. Worse, when environmental groups do suggest solutions, they tend to be presented as duties – we are given lists of things we must not do, joys we must surrender. This can be counter-productive.

In recognizing what drives *us*, we must accept that other people too are more likely to pursue personal interests rather than duty. So the great challenge is to make duty coincide with personal interest. To ask: how can we make doing the right thing *appealing*, rather than merely necessary?

If we want to get people to help us in our projects, we should create a movement for change that provides an opportunity for community and togetherness. And to do this we need to identify social benefits as well as purely technical and financial ones.

When environmentalists lecture us about the need to save the planet, they sometimes emphasize the importance of saving strangers in distant lands, or the generations that will come after us. Alas, the very distance of these 'other people' works against any attempt to motivate us to help them: we just can't get excited about saving the livelihoods of people we've never met and cannot even picture. Humans are deeply sociable creatures, and will seize the chance to help others – but our capacity to do this depends on an imaginative engagement that is hard to sustain over great distances of time or place.

When environmental initiatives have been life-enhancing, even fun, they have usually allowed people to confront an issue by forging communal bonds around it. The underlying reason for coming together might have been to save the world, but for many of those involved the driver will have been nothing more or less than a desire to be with people. We should never underestimate the value of this social instinct when we try to change things. If we offer people a chance to say hello to their neighbours, our projects will be infinitely more successful.

To understand this, consider the Green Belt Movement founded by Wangari Maathai in Kenya in 1977. It's a non-profit organization that promotes environmental conservation among lower-income rural Kenyan women. The movement's female members have planted more than 45 million trees across their country, thus preventing large stretches of it from turning into shrub and desert. But for the individual women who have been involved in the project, it hasn't just been about reforestation and the alkaline levels in the soil. It is the social side of the movement that has had the most immediate benefit for them and been the greatest motivator of their efforts. They speak of the deep connections they forged during tree-planting sessions with women they might otherwise never have met – and how this communal work, outside of the presence of male relatives in a highly patriarchal Kenyan society, gave them a new confidence and stature.

Perhaps the greatest environmental and economic challenge of our age is the fact that we have substantially depleted our oil reserves, and may even have passed the peak of global production – or, in the language of geologists, that we have entered the era of 'peak oil'.

When we read about this in the abstract, the problem sounds both dreary and chilling – a reason to retreat into ourselves and do nothing in particular besides panic. But some people have found ways to turn this catastrophic prospect into an opportunity to rethink our economic arrangements and, in the process – to the delight of many who've become involved – to adjust how we relate to our neighbours and make new friends.

The Transition Town movement was launched in England in 2005. It's a grassroots organization of volunteers that spread by word of mouth to towns and villages around the country. The people involved – there is no official membership – devote themselves to preparing, with thought and imagination, for the day when the world will need to get by with considerably less oil – a world in which transport and much that depends on it will be prohibitively expensive. Rather than presenting this as a disaster, the Transition Town movement stresses the possibilities that will arise as people start to think more ecologically and locally – growing food in their own locality, building homes that are less wasteful of energy, and supporting their local economy as much as possible.

It's hard to see how to be upbeat about a world in which energy will be so scarce, but the Transition Town network is founded on the notion of finding an upside in the combined threat of peak oil and climate change. 'Realistically, only a very small percentage of people will think that life beyond abundant oil could be preferable to what we have now,' one of the founders of the Transition movement, Rob Hopkins, told me. 'But I don't think it has to be a dark age. It could be a most extraordinary renaissance.'

It has to be admitted that, when they first read up about the facts around oil, Hopkins and his allies went through something like the classic grief cycle described by the psychiatrist Elisabeth Kübler-Ross – from despair to anger, then bargaining, depression and finally acceptance – before they were able to be so optimistic. Realizing that most other people have not gone through that – and don't want to – Transition Towns try to find ways to nudge society towards more sustainable practices *that are also fun*.

To begin, Hopkins and his allies used a technique that we could all use to find motivation, whatever our mission of change: they sent themselves, in effect, a cheerful postcard from the future. They used 'imaginary hindsight' to picture what the world could be like in a hundred years if humankind gets it mostly right – and they concluded that local communities will all be much more self-sufficient than today, and more close-knit.

Then they worked out, backwards, how to get there, year by year. The steps for change included: teach people to grow food and make and mend clothes (and other items), hold workshops to give energy-conservation advice, and form clubs to install renewable-power facilities. In each case, as these strategies were put into practice, the leaders of the movement found out something remarkable: that people actually enjoyed coming together with a common purpose, picking up useful and engaging skills and (in the process) building a greater sense of community.

When I first found out about 'peak oil', in 2005, I was desperately worried. I told my wife that the future as we had always imagined it was an illusion. (This didn't go down very well.) I wanted to act, but felt lost until I heard about the startlingly upbeat approach of Hopkins and the other Transition pioneers. I happened to tell friends about Transition, and was thrilled when one of them asked me to help him set up a group in his area, near where I live. (See how bearing witness, on its own, can pull us into being a part of what we observe and tell others about.) Soon others joined us, and it was enormously reassuring to see that people shared our concern.

The high point was a meeting in a crowded hall in north London. Hoping to spread awareness, and find allies, we had invited everybody we could think of who might have an interest in joining forces: local members of environmental lobby groups, people who promote fair trade, church groups, members of the local barter network, political parties, as well as anybody else who lived locally. We explained what we were doing, and then – as Chris Johnstone recommends – explicitly asked for help.

In the months that followed, our group achieved a great deal, organizing film screenings, talks and even a street fair. But I was impatient to do more than preach to the converted. With peak oil and climate change looking increasingly menacing, I wanted to see *everybody* growing their own food. What to do?

My next step was substantially inspired by a book called *Soil and Soul*, by Alastair McIntosh, who has been involved in extremely successful community groups in Scotland. A practising Christian, McIntosh has written about the imperative to re-imagine and act upon the old Christian dictum to love your neighbour. When it comes to trying to change the world, he has argued, it's no good campaigners shouting through a megaphone at anonymous millions. They must start with those closest to them. If they are not good neighbours, then why should anybody listen?

I was powerfully struck by this point. Transition Towns emphasize local engagement, and McIntosh took that to the logical conclusion: I would try to work with my neighbours. And not just the handful of people in my street who might be inclined towards environmentalism already, but my actual next-door neighbours.

I had moved into my house a few years earlier, and knew Martin and Val enough to say hello and have little chats. (The house on the other side was empty.) We'd been into each other's houses, but not often or for long. We looked after each other's spare keys. I hadn't the faintest idea what they thought about peak oil.

So I walked round one afternoon and knocked on the door, which was opened by Val. I told her I had got hold of a film about how the world was going to run out of oil soon, and I wondered if they might like to pop round and watch it one day – any day. How were they fixed next week?

This may not have been the most attractive invitation Martin and Val ever received, but to their eternal credit they said they'd like to come round the following Tuesday afternoon. They would bring a friend too, Val said, if that was alright, because she was interested in that kind of thing.

So the day came, and I bought some biscuits and made tea and we watched the film, *A Crude Awakening*, which is pretty devastating, because it destroys all possibility of the future we might previously have hoped for. I was a bit worried about this, because, as Raymond Williams put it, the key thing is not to make despair convincing.

Afterwards we had a little chat. I can't remember exactly what we said. But a few weeks later workmen came round and installed solar panels on Martin and Val's roof.

I was stunned. This loving-your-neighbour business was more powerful than I could have imagined. I had learned for myself that it's possible to extend your support network into unexpected places.

To be clear, I don't mean to suggest that we think of our neighbours as merely *useful*. At every moment, we choose to see others either as people like ourselves, or as objects in our own life's drama. They either count like we do, or they don't. I'm glad to report that Martin and Val counted very much. In fact, with hindsight, I think I am less pleased by their installation of renewable energy than by the fact that they agreed to come and watch a rather unpromising film; and that Martin subsequently invited me to lunch. Simone Weil once wrote that the sense of being rooted is a greatly overlooked human need – and, as I found, getting to know your neighbours is a great way to feel more rooted.

I wondered if I might get any more locals involved in my positive change. That September, I collected apples from my apple tree and put them in a huge box, which I carried under one arm while holding my young daughter's hand in my other hand. We walked up and down the street, telling our neighbours we had more apples than we could use, and would they like some? I had calculated that a man holding a toddler's hand, and offering fruit at no cost, is not unduly frightening. Most neighbours seemed glad to take a handful of apples.

A few months later, I sowed dozens of tomato seeds in small pots. When the young plants appeared, I got hold of another box, grabbed my daughter's hand, and went up and down the street again. I told my neighbours I had grown 'too many' tomato seedlings. Oh dear! Would they like one? Nobody refused, and that year, several people in my street enjoyed growing their own food for the first time. Perhaps they were going to do that anyway – but I like to think I gave them a little push – and without even mentioning peak oil.

Your ideas for changing the world may feel desperately important. They may *be* desperately important. But if you can't find a way to engage the interests of the people around you – including your next-door neighbours – they may never take off.

And perhaps they don't deserve to.

Grown too many vegetables? Leave them on your neighbours' doorsteps, and next year they might grow their own.

4. Love Helps

As we grow more comfortable engaging with other people, and building a stronger community, we eventually come up against individuals who are difficult, not merely apathetic and resistant to our themes, but burdened with problems of their own, including personal problems that can make them very hard to engage with and can lead to them being marginalized in the community.

Instinctively, we may wish we could avoid these kinds of people, because dealing with them can be extremely hard work, but dealing with them teaches us an important lesson; that we may be better equipped, as individuals, to deal with social problems than governments or other official bodies. That's because state agencies, when they're confronted by social problems, usually respond by throwing money – it is difficult for them to act in any other way.

But not all people's needs are material. Sometimes what is really needed is help of a more personal kind. Sometimes what is needed is love.

No one needs this more than children, whatever their background. It's in the care of children that we see the limitations of purely cash-based assistance. Somebody who knows a great deal about this is Camila Batmanghelidjh, a woman who worked for years as a nanny in rich but sometimes troubled or neglectful families, but also has extensive qualifications in psychotherapy and has in recent years helped London's most impoverished children through her own pioneering charity, Kids Company.

Many of the children's individual stories are heartbreaking, but the really shocking thing is the sheer *number* of children involved: Kids Company has thousands on its files. They include the sort of young people we might cross the street to avoid – and with good reason, because despite their age many have been involved in violent crime. But Batmanghelidjh is plainly happy among them. Meeting her is to be confronted with the possibility of a totally different way of thinking.

Many of the children come from severely impoverished homes. In fact, 85 per cent would not have an evening meal if it weren't for Kids Company. But having seen dysfunction in rich homes, too, Batmanghelidjh knows that the childrens' problems are not *only* financial. 'I saw terrible neglect in those homes,' she told me. Money alone can't give children what they need most.

Underlying everything Kids Company does is a belief in love. In particular, the organization is indebted to what is known as Attachment Theory, which was first elaborated by the child-psychologist John Bowlby. This essentially holds that children develop as the direct result of how their first carers engage with them. Physically and emotionally neglected children expect others to be unresponsive, unavailable, and unwilling to meet their needs. Abused children expect others to be rejecting, hostile, and unavailable. Both types behave in ways that increase the likelihood that others will treat them in the ways they expect. And once a child has established a model of its relationships, Bowlby suggested, changing it can be difficult.

Fortunately, not all is lost if early love was missing. A study by the University of Minnesota showed that 61 per cent of mothers who had been sexually abused as children went on to maltreat their own children. However, the same study found that the availability of emotionally supportive individuals and involvement in long-term, intensive psychotherapy could substantially reduce the chances of the repetition of abuse. And that is precisely what children get from Kids Company.

Many of these children have lost the ability to empathize. It's no good merely instructing them in conventional morality. If troubled children are to care for others, they first need to hear someone apologize to them for everything they've been through. Kids Company staff do that: they apologize. Then they attempt to remodel children's ability to empathize by helping them to form intensive-attachment relationships with trained adults.

It would be a mistake to suppose this process goes smoothly. At first, the children often become more aggressive, not less. 'They don't want that attachment to develop,' Batmanghelidjh told me. 'They say we are making them soft, and they won't be able to survive on the streets.' But eventually most of the children are turned around.

I once spent several months observing Kids Company at work. Some of the children I met had been extremely troubled. One was a girl who used to be uncontrollably wild, and would stop on the street to pick fights with strangers. Through the loving care of Kids Company workers, Cleo had learned to stop doing that. Indeed, staff had recently started taking her to restaurants, to learn things that would not otherwise be in her behavioural repertoire – from engaging with waiters to holding the cutlery correctly. Another time, the invitation to dine out came from the children: Batmanghelidjh was taken out by a group of young immigrants, formerly child soldiers, who had just been granted places at university and wanted to repay her years of kindness with a pizza.

We don't need to set up a charity to make a difference of this kind. We could volunteer to help somebody like Batmanghelidjh who has already done that – or just decide to do something ourselves.

That's what Fenella Rouse did. 'It started with me and my hair-dresser,' Rouse told me. 'We were talking about things that need to be done, and what could we do ourselves. And we were struck by the number of young people who aren't in paid employment.'

Resolving to act, Rouse walked into a jobcentre near her home in north London and announced that she'd like to help some young people to find work. (She had recently reached retirement age, and had a bit of spare time.) She said she particularly wanted to help youngsters with no qualifications, and no family tradition of work. A government-funded jobcentre could not afford to overlook the lack of qualifications, but Rouse, a mother of young adults herself, knew that formal qualifications aren't everything.

The jobcentre staff suggested a few names, and Rouse approached the young people. She told them what she wanted to do, explaining that she would try to find them placements with her friends, or in offices that seemed interested in helping.

It was immediately apparent to the young people that this was a woman offering nothing but kindness. They accepted it.

The work proved to be more time-consuming than Rouse expected. She travelled far across the city to meet the young people's families. She also found it necessary to collect them from home and accompany them all the way to the workplace, on the first day, having learnt by experience that, no matter how confident they sounded beforehand, not one of them was able to find their way around London by public transport. She also gave pep talks, and explained basic office conduct. (Some young people needed to be told during their placements not to spend so much time arranging their social lives when they were at work.) One or two of the youngsters panicked, leaving their placement early and never going back. Rouse would phone them several times before they eventually took her call. She gently told them they would look back on this as the moment they decided to stop letting themselves down. And that's what happened: one girl having been thus gently rebuked, went out to find a new job herself and thrived in it.

Like Batmanghelidjh, Rouse was motivated by love to help young people who badly needed it. Unlike Batmanghelidjh, she did not set up an organization, with staff and premises and other overheads. She was just an individual, with a mobile phone. But she almost single-handedly transformed the prospects of several 'unemployable' youngsters by finding work placements that led to real jobs.

One of the young people she helped said to me, afterwards, 'She's a lovely person. Anyone could try to do what she has done, but to be able to get along with people like she does . . . She's one of a kind.'

But Rouse doesn't see herself as unique. 'Anyone could do what I've done,' she says modestly, 'if they like young people and have a bit of spare time.'

Being short of money can seem to let us off the hook: we'd dearly like to help, but economic circumstances won't allow us. But Rouse and Batmanghelidjh show that true generosity consists of more than writing a cheque, or putting coins in a tin. And the resource they distribute is one we all have in abundance. It may not be in our power to build new schools, but it is definitely always an option to give our care, attention and love.

5. Aim for a Peace Prize

When we want to change the world, we frequently realize early on that there are groups of people who are standing in our way. And typically we respond by categorizing them as The Enemy – pure evil in contrast to our own perceived purity – and we set about trying to overcome them in whatever way we can: by defeating them in an election, outsmarting them at a dinner party, mocking them in a newspaper article, punching them in the stomach or killing them in battle. We associate getting our way, and forcing through the benevolent change we are looking for, with being able to vanquish The Enemy.

Much of the change the world has seen in its history has come through violent conquest of one kind or another. But there are plenty of examples, which I want to highlight, of remarkable changes that have come about when two camps learn to see each other as legitimate human agents who hold positions which, while divergent from their own, are not intrinsically evil or worthy of being trampled upon.

The other day, in a left-of-centre newspaper that usually opposes war and violence, I read an article written by a woman who supports Britain's Labour party. The identity of the writer doesn't matter, and nor does the specific point of her article. It's just an article I happened to read. I was shocked by the quantity of warlike language in it. The headline urged Labour to 'take the fight' to the Conservative government, 'day in, day out', to use their 'considerable fire power' for 'daily cannonades', to 'deliver smart bombs' and devote themselves to 'devastatingly forensic attacks', in order to 'knock the hell out of government'.

Nobody was physically harmed by the article and I'm sure the writer would have been appalled if Labour politicians did start dropping bombs. But to write in this way is to dehumanize the government, and the individuals within it. We hear similar things in conversation every day.

If we agree with them, rallying cries like this make us feel like part of a select group and capable of great action. But it also sets us up as 'against' the rest of the world – including people we may need to convince if we want to make a difference. So one way to make a difference is to start to take these small but significant examples of dehumanization seriously; if we want to live in a less violent world, we could write letters to people like that newspaper writer and, in the gentlest ways, ask if she might reduce the use of bellicose metaphor a little in the interests of making positive change. And we might try not to use the same kind of language ourselves.

The need to halt our dehumanizing impulses is never more urgent than when it comes to the threat of armed conflict. Those who've worked most closely with warring parties tend to report a small but fascinating truth: if you get them into the same room, get them to have a meal together, shake hands, look into each other's eyes or take a walk together, you have a much higher chance of resolving conflict than by merely holding debates in parliament or calling for UN troops. It's those gestures that remind each party of the other's fundamental humanity that are key to any attempt to make peace take hold.

A famous example of this kind of re-humanization took place in what was then Rhodesia, at the time of its transition to Zimbabwe in 1980. Fighting had been going on for years between blacks and whites. Under white minority rule the government, led by Ian Smith, had unilaterally declared Rhodesia independent of Britain in 1965. Sanctions by Britain and the UN followed, while internally the country was riven by guerilla war. Killings, torture, rape and pillage became common and one in six of the black population were displaced. Some twenty initiatives had been made to establish peace – to no effect – when the parties agreed, at a conference in London, to hold an election. Whatever the result of the election, few expected peace to follow. The head of the armed forces was understood to have prepared a coup in case it went against the white minority, while African nationalists confided years later that they had been waiting 'to kill every white in sight' if the order were given.

Fortunately, the disaster that could have occurred was averted in the simplest way possible: Smith and Robert Mugabe got together in the same room and had a drink together. A group of citizens, both white and black, realized what was in danger of ensuing after the election and persuaded Smith to meet Mugabe at his headquarters. As Smith walked in, he passed fifty heavily armed guards. One shouted out 'Let's get rid of him now!' and raised his gun at Smith – only to be sent sprawling by one of his own commanders. Inside, something extraordinary happened that we might think about whenever we are confronting a seemingly intractable problem within our own social circle: Mugabe invited his former enemy to sit beside him on a couch and for several hours they talked about themselves and their love and hopes for their country. In other words, they found a context in which

Bitter enemies: but a private meeting between Ian Smith and Robert Mugabe
enabled them to make terms.

to realize they were both human. They both knew Mugabe was likely to win. He outlined the policies he intended to pursue, and stressed his eagerness to retain the confidence of the white population. He asked Smith what measures might be necessary, and offered him two cabinet seats. Immediately after Mugabe was declared winner, Smith announced that he accepted the results, had met Mugabe and he had found him to be a 'reasonable man'. Smith added that he intended to stay in the country and recommended that other white people do the same. That evening, Mugabe addressed the nation. 'I urge you,' he said, 'whether you are black or white to join me in a new phase and to forget our grave past. Forgive others and forget.'

It sounds simple, but neither Mugabe nor Smith had felt able to call for this kind of meeting without losing face. They needed outsiders, unaffiliated with either side, to do it for them. Reading this years later, you may feel confused. Is this a story about Robert Mugabe as peacemaker? The recent history of Zimbabwe makes such a possibility hard to believe. Surely Mugabe is a monster? But what happened in Rhodesia is instructive because it shows that change is possible even in the most unlikely circumstances. We don't get to choose the people who pose a problem – they're just there. We might feel more comfortable reading about peace breaking out elsewhere, with more attractive protagonists. But resolving conflict is not about making even closer friends with people who already behave nicely. We may one day have to deal with individuals who behave like monsters. It's more startling, and more impressive, to learn that somebody like Mugabe could be persuaded to make peace. It starts to put our own quarrels and disagreements into perspective.

If we are going to find lasting solutions to external conflict, we first need to find a way out of the internal conflicts that poison our thoughts, feelings and attitudes towards others. No conflict can ever be solved so long as all parties are convinced they are right. A solution is only possible when at least one begins to consider how he or she might be wrong. And the deepest way in which we tend to be right or wrong is not in the intellectual positions we adopt but the attitude we have towards the other person. If we don't respect them as a person with real interests and vulnerabilities of their own, we will get nowhere.

We also have to realize that we may not get everything we want, but we can get something more than we'd feared. Peter Emerson has devoted his life to promoting peace by championing this kind of realism. His ideas have been tested in conflict zones such as Bosnia and Emerson's native Northern Ireland, a territory long divided by armed violence between sectarian groups. Emerson promotes a decision-making process that, rather than entrenching division, works towards consensus and shared interests. The system was originally conceived in pre-revolutionary France, by a scientist called Jean-Charles de Borda. Because it relies on complex maths, it was hard to put into practice until the advent of computers. But the Borda count, or 'preferendum', will be familiar to anybody who has ever watched the Eurovision Song Contest: voters simply express their preference on a range of options, ranking them from highest to lowest. The winning option may not have been any individual voter's first choice, but will have won higher overall approval than any other option. The losing option, though it may have been some voters' first choice, will have the lowest overall approval. The multi-option preferendum can be used either to elect individuals or to choose between policies. It can be used in formal politics, but also among friends, in clubs or at the office. Whatever the context, people usually have the same basic interests, Emerson says, but in a different order of priority. The preferendum allows them to recognize this. They may not agree on each other's first choice, but will quickly agree on the second or third.

What is particularly interesting about Emerson's experience is that adopting a different technique for finding common ground can change the way individuals regard people they formerly saw as opponents. They start to see them as more like colleagues. This is because, in the preferendum, nobody votes *against* anything. Instead, you vote for every option, but in your own order of preference. No matter how strongly voters disagree, they must give at least one point to those of an opposite persuasion. 'The effect of having to accept literally everyone as a neighbour may make an incalculable contribution towards mutual understanding and accommodation,' says Emerson. 'Every individual starts the reconciliation process . . . with himself.' If someone wants a particular policy to be adopted, he or she must persuade not only the mild supporter to become more committed, and give 9 or 10 points instead of just 6 or 7 – but also the opponent must be warmed a little, to give 6 or 7 instead of 1 or 2. Rather than merely preach to the converted, there is more to be gained by gently wooing those who would previously have been seen as political adversaries, and ignored. Thus the very use of a consensual system will in itself promote consensus, both in the course of a civilized debate and in the resolutions that may follow.

Eventually, as people discover their common interests, they find themselves able to overlook differences that previously seemed so important. In Northern Ireland, a consequence of this is that previously bitter enemies like the loyalist Ian Paisley and the nationalist Martin McGuinness are able to work together successfully.

What is going on here is essentially an unfolding of compassion. Individuals are starting to see things from the other's point of view. The writer (and former nun) Karen Armstrong believes that compassion is the key to changing the world. In 2008, Armstrong was awarded the TED Prize for her work in this area over many years. At the award ceremony, she asked TED to help her create, launch and propagate a Charter for Compassion, to be written by leading thinkers from a variety of major faiths around the world. The charter was launched the following year.

Compassion does not mean 'to feel sorry for somebody' (a mistake Armstrong frequently encounters). It means to endure something with another person, to put ourselves in somebody else's shoes, to feel his or her pain as though it were our own, and enter generously into his or her point of view. Every faith insists on compassion as the true test of spirituality, and has a version of the so-called Golden Rule, which requires us to treat others as we would like to be treated by them, and not to treat them in ways we would find unwelcome. And we must do this for everybody, including our enemies.

'Sceptics say the Golden Rule just "doesn't work" but they don't seem to have tried it,' Armstrong says. 'It's not a doctrine that you decide either to agree with or not. It's a method, and the only way to test it is to put it into practice.' When people have done this they have reported experiencing deeper, fuller levels of existence – and insisted that anybody could do the same if they tried.

To develop greater levels of compassion, it may be necessary to work on it, like sports professionals in training. There are many exercises we might try. One is to imagine a relative or friend in the place of a person who is suffering. It is hard to disregard a homeless man if you imagine that he might be your father, or your brother or son.

Wishing for your enemy's well-being and happiness is harder. Indeed, Armstrong says, developing a sense of responsibility for your enemy's pain is the supreme test of compassion. At first it may seem impossible. (How can we feel compassion for Robert Mugabe?) If we do manage it, briefly, it is all too easy to fall back into our old ways. The attempt to become compassionate is a lifelong project. Nearly every day we will fail, but we cannot give up.

But the great danger with altruism generated in the seclusion of one's own thoughts is that it might become a subtle means of evading actual interpersonal responsibility, and justify a life of peaceful, uninvolved isolation from others: 'We proclaim to ourselves our love and compassion for such abstract entities as "humanity"', says the Buddhist writer Jack Kornfield, 'in order to avoid having to love any one person.' Or to put that another way, we may be tempted to say we feel love for everybody – but without actually engaging with the real people whom we find difficult or unpleasant.

Which brings me to a story of what happened some years ago between me and a friend, and our own painful falling out. I would like to describe how our dispute arose, and what its consequences were.

I mention this in the context of armed conflicts because it is petty every-day resentments that, if they're left unchecked, grow into cold hatred, then violence. If nothing is done to dismantle these resentments, they may even lead to bombing campaigns. Or, expressed differently: large-scale violence always grows out of private resentments.

I had known Paul since childhood. From as early as either of us could remember, we were very close – like brothers. But he grew up to be a big drinker, and when he was drunk tended to be very unpleasant. We would have tetchy conversations, in which he said things that were unreasonable. Instead of ignoring them or laughing them off, I argued back. At the time, this seemed the right approach: here was a man wasting his life drinking and he needed to be put right. In short, we wound each other up – inviting the very behaviours we hated in each other. (This is why conflict-resolution specialists speak of enemies as being in collusion, rather than merely in conflict.)

I can't remember now exactly what caused me eventually to lose my temper, one evening soon after Christmas, but it started with his accusation that I was not sufficiently grateful for a gift. He was very drunk, he was shouting, and then – I'm ashamed to say that I punched him in the stomach before I knew what I was doing.

We hardly spoke for three years afterwards. You might think I was better off without him, but we had always been close, and our estrangement was a lingering shadow over my daily life. It was painful for people who knew us, too. It would be neat if I could say that one of those other people brought us together – like Mugabe and Smith. Only the situation isn't quite the same. Mugabe and Smith needed third-party assistance because, as leaders of a wider movement, neither man could risk losing face by reaching out to the other and being rebuffed. Private disputes between individuals are different. When you don't represent anybody else, it's easier to take that kind of risk yourself.

But if you are waiting for me to reveal that I reached out to him, and nobly set about putting our relationship in order, I'm afraid I can't do that, because it was Paul who reached out to me.

In doing so, he made it possible for me to feel compassion for him. In fact, I think it would have been very hard, in the circumstances, *not* to show compassion.

It was a Saturday afternoon. He was at a football match. He told me he'd been out drinking all night, in a park. Then he said he'd had enough. He mentioned his recent divorce, and spending his birthday alone. And at the top of his voice – shouting to be heard over the din of the football crowd – he said he was going to kill himself.

Before he called, I had carried resentment and hostility towards him. I resented his drinking particularly. Now he was calling and he was obviously very drunk. But it was clear that his call for help was sincere, and this had a powerful effect: in an instant, I became his old friend again. I have since met people who work in restorative justice who tell me this kind of thing happens often: criminals brought to meet their victims may break down in tears – and victims are surprised to find themselves moved to help the criminals put their lives on the right track. I'm not suggesting that Paul and I were criminal and victim – it was I who hit him, not the other way round – but his call for help transformed my feelings towards him at a stroke.

I urged him not to do anything rash and after hanging up, I found a phone number for Alcoholics Anonymous. The woman who answered the phone told me Paul must call AA himself.

I drove to see him. I was shocked by the squalor of his home – a single room overlooking a busy main road in a poor district – and the powerful odour of alcohol he gave off, but I tried to hide this feeling. Over the next hour or two, I assured him that I, for one, cared for him and couldn't bear the idea of his suicide – and that I was sure many other friends felt the same way. That was only half-true: his behaviour, over the years, had reduced those 'many other' friends to just a few.

I urged him to call AA, and summarized what I knew about it. As I left, I pressed into Paul's hand AA's phone number, scribbled on a Post-it note.

I doubted that he would call. And for a week, he didn't: people don't always do what we want them to do. But then he did. He went to one meeting, then another. Suddenly he was going every day, and talking at length about AA and its celebrated Twelve-Step program. With support from strangers who have been through a similar experience, he stayed sober for a week, then a month, and now nine years. He met someone else, moved into a house, and they had a child – a little girl.

We are close friends again, and he has since returned the favour by giving me support when I needed it.

I mention this personal story to point out something extremely important: that resolving conflict is not only about making peace between nation states. It's about looking at our own situation, among friends and relatives, and asking if there may be somebody with whom we should try to straighten things out. Because, as I pointed out at the very beginning of this book, the things we tend to think of as historically significant – achievements of the sort credited to Julius Caesar, Genghis Khan and Christopher Columbus – aren't really any more important than the small things we can all do, every day.

IV. Conclusion

In the first part of the book, we saw that we do not need to accept the way things are. In the second part, we looked at a variety of ways to engage with the world and with other people – and, by extension, to cultivate an ever greater sense of community. But these were only examples, and while you were reading this book I hope you will have had your own ideas about how to make a positive change. You may perhaps have had these ideas for a long time. In which case, you must do something about them.

Before you start, a final word of caution. We need to accept that even our best efforts will have unintended consequences, and may even be harmful.

To give an example: the 'Green Revolution' in agriculture enabled farmers to increase massively the amount of food they grew, and thus saved many people from starvation. Norman Borlaug, one of the scientists most closely involved, was given a Nobel prize for his work. But the very success of this scientific approach to food-growing made it possible for the global population to reach unsustainable proportions. Likewise, the inventor of the motor car indirectly made it possible for humankind to emit the most incredible quantity of carbon dioxide into the atmosphere. Trade unions that improved wages and working conditions may thereby have pushed employers to export jobs overseas. The creators of financial instruments that vastly improved liquidity inadvertently contributed towards an international financial system that poses a threat to the world economy.

The list could go on. But the point is not to be clever at the expense of people who almost certainly believed themselves to be doing something of real value (and not only for themselves). If we had been in their shoes and had their capabilities, we would probably have done the same, and accepted the plaudits of people who told us we were changing the world in a good way.

The fact is that *anything* we do might be characterized as unhelpful, if only by people far away from ourselves, in time or space, who must deal with consequences that are hidden from us. Being aware of this, we are less likely to get carried away with messianic zeal, and that's no bad thing. In changing the world, we can proceed with a degree of humility.

But this awareness does not stop us from acting. It merely reinforces the importance of the here and now. If we can foresee problems likely to be caused by our actions, we should of course draw back and think again, but if we sincerely can't imagine what those problems may be, we should humbly accept that they might arise, hope that somebody else will think of a way to deal with them when the time comes, and get on with doing whatever needs to be done *now*.

And if we are to do anything, we need first to accept that we can't fix *everything*. When we accept that, we allow ourselves to stop feeling daunted by the scale of what we hope to achieve. This kind of anxiety is understandable, but unnecessary. 'Nobody made a greater mistake than he who did nothing because he could do only a little', said Edmund Burke, the Irish statesman.

Change the world by doing what you can. Rob 'The Rubbish' Kevan picks up the litter near his Welsh home town every day.

If we make the mistake Burke describes, we're likely to postpone action, deluding ourselves that we will do our great works at a later date, when circumstances are more favourable – when we get a new job, perhaps, or move to a bigger house, or retire.

When we wish for the landscape to change in this way we're using 'static' thinking: imagining our goals as, essentially, finished paintings, beautifully framed, that we hope one day to hang on our wall. But the trouble is that nobody is doing any painting.

It helps to use 'process' thinking instead. As Nietzsche said, 'Not every end is a goal. The end of a melody is not a goal.' Which is to say: we don't go to a concert and wish that the music would hurry up and finish, so that we can enjoy it. We enjoy it *as it goes along*. So instead of imagining your mission as a painting, think of it as a piece of music. By all means keep an eye on the long term. (Indeed, you must, if you're to know where you are going. Nietzsche continued: '. . . If the melody had not reached its end it would not have reached its goal either.') But having identified your long-term target, focus on the present. Ask yourself: what can I do in the next 24 hours? Because if you don't do anything in 24 hours, what makes you think you ever will?

If Wangari Maathai had not focused on the small steps, her group would never have planted all those millions of trees: 'Until you dig a hole, you plant a tree, you water it and make it survive, you haven't done a thing,' she said. 'You are just talking.'

Mother Teresa of Calcutta took much the same view: 'I never look at the masses as my responsibility,' she said. 'I look at the individual. I can only love one person at a time, just one, one, one. I began, I picked up one person. Maybe if I didn't pick up that one person, I wouldn't have picked up 42,000. The whole work is only a drop in the ocean. But if I didn't put the drop in, the ocean would be one drop less.'

Nobody ever achieved anything except in small steps, one after another. That stone mason who built the magnificent cathedral for others to enjoy, long after he'd gone, did so exactly like his colleagues: by squaring off stones and moving them – again and again and again.

Small actions are important. Sufis teach that every act can be done for the Beloved. Others might choose to fold laundry as if it were the robes of Jesus or Buddha. Gandhi called these small acts 'blessed monotony'. His own great achievements developed slowly, and we know that he frequently sought reassurance from a passage in the Baghavad Gita, in which Lord Krishna urges us to practice karma yoga – to do work independently of the anticipated outcome.

If we follow this advice, removing our focus from the end, a happy result is that we are less likely to use the end to justify questionable means. We make each step enjoyable and valuable in its own right. And by focusing properly on the small steps, we come to recognize them as what they are: mini-victories, each one giving us confidence to move on to the next challenge – just as protesters in Montgomery, Alabama, moved, gradually, from calling for minor changes to the rules about who sits where on local buses to demanding an end to segregation entirely; a previously unthinkable ambition.

It's worth building a time into your schedule to focus on the mini-victories properly, and recognize their true worth. Make an appointment to ask yourself, at the end of each week, what you have achieved – and what you are looking forward to next week. This modest practice will benefit anybody.

As you notice how much you have achieved, you may wish to raise your longer-term ambitions. But be careful not to get too wrapped up in thinking of those small steps only as a part of something bigger. Really enjoy them *in their own right*.

The principles in this book will only work if they come from the heart. What is proposed is not a bag of tricks, but a new way of living. If you are genuinely interested in forming new habits, keep this book nearby after you have finished it and look through it again every so often. Ask yourself what you have done recently that you might have done better, but also make a note of the things you did well. Actually write down your triumphs, with specific details. Because it is those details, as much as any stories you find written in here, that will give you the courage to go even further.

Changing the world is a job that never ends. In that sense, it's not so much a job as a state of mind: attentive to the way things are, willing to share responsibility for it, and determined not to make despair convincing, but hope possible.

People engaged in this work try to look for the upside, find resources where others might overlook them, and recognize allies in sometimes unexpected places. They focus on the long term but always think how to take small actions right now. They are compassionate and even humble, but experience life as an adventure, rather than a series of oppressive incidents entirely beyond their control. And rather than complain that the work never ends, they see reason to be glad: because there will always be something else to do.

You can be one of them.

Homework

A very large number of books, articles, films and conversations contributed towards the ideas in this book. The following were very useful, not only in the chapters where they are first cited – and are all highly recommended.

II. How to Start to Make a Change

1. Overcoming Defeatism

Leo Tolstoy wrote essays about the importance of absolutely everybody's actions and omissions but he first became aware of it when writing fiction, particularly the epic *War and Peace*. A similarly hefty volume, with narrative drive and global sweep, is *A Force More Powerful*, Peter Ackerman and Jack DuVall's compendium of non-violent campaigns in the last century or so. Gene Sharp's magnum opus, *The Politics of Non-Violent Action*, is more academic but it's hard not to be impressed by the breadth of his research, and the force of his case that power is enjoyed only by the consent of those over whom it is exercised. Of course, he got the idea from Gandhi, whose own writings were extensive: you could start with *The Story of My Experiments With Truth*. For an English-language account of the group that did so much to rattle the Nazis, do read Annette Dumbach and Jud Newborn's *Sophie Scholl and The White Rose*.

2. *What Drives Us?*

The idea of a life well lived is a cornerstone of philosophy, psychology and every religious tradition. In *How Are We To Live?* Peter Singer gives a broad overview of the philosophical ideas, with many challenging insights of his own. You may also want to look into the original writings of Immanuel Kant, David Hume, Albert Camus, Jean-Paul Sartre, and Iris Murdoch. Viktor Frankl, Martin Seligman and Chris Johnstone provide extremely practical ideas from psychology and other clinical disciplines (and raw personal experience). Of the religious traditions, I rely here mostly on Buddhist writings (though I recommend others too). Stephen Batchelor is a British Buddhist of long-standing: he combines that expertise with existentialist ideas in *Alone With Others*. Thich Nhat Hanh is a Vietnamese monk who has lived in the west for years; *The Heart of the Buddha's Teaching* is clear, and comprehensive, but for a more accessible read try *The Miracle of Mindfulness*. Richard Nelson Bolles' *What Color is Your Parachute?* is written for job-seekers, but contains excellent self-assessment tests.

3. Some Thoughts on Strategy

In *Eradicating Ecocide*, Polly Higgins explains in detail why she thinks a law, like the law against genocide, is needed to protect the planet. Rebecca Solnit's *Hope in the Dark* is less direct, and contains many memorable formulations about change-making. The examples of non-violent techniques are taken from Gene Sharp: it would be wonderful if somebody started a wiki site allowing people all over the world to upload other instances of each technique. The book to read about the Scouts is of course Robert Baden-Powell's *Scouting For Boys* (though things have moved on a bit). The story about the business-men pretending to be hippies is from Keith Johnstone's remarkable book on creativity, *Impro*.

4. Bearing Witness

The place to read about prophets is of course the Bible, though it is less up-to-date than Trenna Cormack's book of interviews with contemporary voices of hope, *Be the Change*. Jung Chang's memoir about a family in China, *Wild Swans*, is painful to read but gripping, and illustrates just how badly things can go wrong if people don't recognize their own power to effect change. Precisely the opposite effect is achieved by Dale Carnegie's *How To Win Friends And Influence People* – a book that is easy to mock until you actually read it. The advice it contains is practical, upbeat and relentless.

5. *What You Will Need*

Richard Reynolds has written a lovely book about his exploits, *On Guerilla Gardening*. To find out more about how Peace Direct supports former child soldiers in their new roles, see www.peacedirect.org

6. *Taking a First Step*

The exercise used by Joanna Macy is mentioned in her book with Molly Young Brown, *Coming Back to Life*. To find out more about her work and other exercises, see www.joannamacy.net. The man at the music festival can be found dancing eternally on YouTube. The civil-rights struggle is well documented in Gene Sharp's work and in Ackerman and DuVall's *A Force More Powerful*; but the quote from the Women's Political Council is from *The Montgomery Bus Boycott and the Women Who Started it: The Memoir of Jo Ann Gibson Robinson*, and Diane Nash's quote is from Catherine Ingram's *In The Footsteps of Gandhi*.

III. What Needs Changing, and How

1. *Add Beauty – and Fun*

Rachael Matthews' blogs at www.prickyourfinger.com. Do give yourself plenty of time to look around www.learningtoloveyoumore.com if you are really to appreciate the hundreds of submissions from around the world. (They're not accepting any more, but that needn't stop you from having a go.)

2. How Does Money Fit In?

Dale Vince, founder of Ecotricity, blogs at www.zerocarbonista.com.
Toby Ord's website is www.givingwhatwecan.org.

3. Make It Appealing

The insightful and moving autobiography of Wangari Maathai is
Unbowed: One Woman's Story. Rob Hopkins first set out his ideas
in *The Transition Handbook*; *The Transition Companion* brings the
story up to date. He blogs at www.transitionculture.org. After *Soil
and Soul*, Alastair McIntosh published the equally inspiring *Hell and
High Water*.

4. Love Helps

Camila Batmanghelidjh has written a powerful, but academically
robust account of her work with several young people, *Shattered Lives*.

5. Aim for a Peace Prize

The story of Ian Smith's secret meeting with Robert Mugabe is told
by Ron Kraybill in Douglas Johnstone and Cynthia Sampson's fascinating *Religion: The Missing Dimension Of Statecraft*. If you want to find
out more about the organization that inspired it, Moral Re-Armament,

it has changed its name to Initiatives of Change (www.iofc.org). Peter Emerson's ideas about consensus voting systems are promoted through the de Borda Institute (www.deborda.org). Karen Armstrong's book, *Twelve Steps to a Compassionate Life* borrows the Twelve Step framework from Alcoholics Anonymous (www.aa.org), which was itself substantially inspired by Moral Re-Armament. Jack Kornfield's quote is from his book *After the Ecstasy, the Laundry*.

Appendix

This list is an excerpt from Gene Sharp's *The Politics of Nonviolent Action, Part II: The Methods of Nonviolent Action,* Boston: Porter Sargent, 1973, available for purchase at www.extendinghorizons.com. The book contains detailed descriptions and historical examples of each of the methods.

198 Ways to Act

The following menu of non-violent actions was drawn up by Gene Sharp over a period of several decades. It is known to have been influential in several non-violent revolutions – but also less dramatic social, artistic and political change.

Raising Awareness/Protest

FORMAL STATEMENTS
1. Public Speeches
2. Letters of opposition or support
3. Declarations by organizations and institutions

4. Signed public statements
5. Declarations of indictment and intention
6. Group or mass petitions

COMMUNICATIONS WITH A WIDER AUDIENCE

7. Slogans, caricatures, and symbols
8. Banners, posters, and displayed communications
9. Leaflets, pamphlets, and books
10. Newspapers and journals
11. Records, radio, and television
12. Sky-writing and earth-writing

GROUP REPRESENTATIONS

13. Deputations
14. Mock awards
15. Group lobbying
16. Picketing
17. Mock elections

SYMBOLIC PUBLIC ACTS

18. Displays of flags and symbolic colours
19. Wearing of symbols
20. Prayer and worship
21. Delivering symbolic objects
22. Protest disrobings
23. Destruction of own property
24. Symbolic lights
25. Displays of portraits

26. Paint as protest
27. New signs and names
28. Symbolic sounds
29. Symbolic reclamations
30. Rude gestures

PRESSURES ON INDIVIDUALS

31. 'Haunting' officials
32. Taunting officials
33. Fraternization
34. Vigils

DRAMA AND MUSIC

35. Humorous skits and pranks
36. Performances of plays and music
37. Singing

PROCESSIONS

38. Marches
39. Parades
40. Religious processions
41. Pilgrimages
42. Motorcades

HONOURING THE DEAD

43. Political mourning
44. Mock funerals
45. Demonstrative funerals
46. Homage at burial places

PUBLIC ASSEMBLIES

47. Assemblies of protest or support
48. Protest meetings
49. Camouflaged meetings of protest
50. Teach-ins

WITHDRAWAL AND RENUNCIATION

51. Walk-outs
52. Silence
53. Renouncing honours
54. Turning one's back

Non-Cooperation

OSTRACISM OF PERSONS

55. Social boycott
56. Selective social boycott
57. Lysistratic non-action (withholding sex)
58. Excommunication
59. Interdict

NON-COOPERATION WITH SOCIAL EVENTS, CUSTOMS, AND INSTITUTIONS

60. Suspension of social and sports activities
61. Boycott of social affairs
62. Student strike
63. Social disobedience
64. Withdrawal from social institutions

WITHDRAWAL FROM THE SOCIAL SYSTEM

65. Stay-at-home
66. Total personal non-cooperation
67. 'Flight' of workers
68. Sanctuary
69. Collective disappearance
70. Protest emigration (*hijrat*)

ACTIONS BY CONSUMERS

71. Consumers' boycott
72. Non-consumption of boycotted goods
73. Policy of austerity
74. Rent withholding
75. Refusal to rent
76. National consumers' boycott
77. International consumers' boycott

ACTION BY WORKERS AND PRODUCERS

78. Workmen's boycott
79. Producers' boycott

ACTION BY MIDDLEMEN

80. Suppliers' and handlers' boycott

ACTION BY OWNERS AND MANAGEMENT

81. Traders' boycott
82. Refusal to let or sell property
83. Lockout

84. Refusal of industrial assistance
85. Merchants' 'general strike'

ACTION BY HOLDERS OF FINANCIAL RESOURCES
86. Withdrawal of bank deposits
87. Refusal to pay fees, dues, and assessments
88. Refusal to pay debts or interest
89. Severance of funds and credit
90. Revenue refusal
91. Refusal of a government's money

ACTION BY GOVERNMENTS
92. Domestic embargo
93. Blacklisting of traders
94. International sellers' embargo
95. International buyers' embargo
96. International trade embargo

SYMBOLIC STRIKES
97. Protest strike
98. Quickie walkout (lightning strike)

AGRICULTURAL STRIKES
99. Peasant strike
100. Farm Workers' strike

STRIKES BY SPECIAL GROUPS
101. Refusal of impressed labour
102. Prisoners' strike

103. Craft strike
104. Professional strike

ORDINARY INDUSTRIAL STRIKES
105. Establishment strike
106. Industry strike
107. Sympathetic strike

RESTRICTED STRIKES
108. Detailed strike
109. Bumper strike
110. Slowdown strike
111. Working-to-rule strike
112. Reporting 'sick' (sick-in)
113. Strike by resignation
114. Limited strike
115. Selective strike

MULTI-INDUSTRY STRIKES
116. Generalized strike
117. General strike

COMBINATION OF STRIKES AND ECONOMIC CLOSURES
118. Hartal, or total civic shutdown
119. Economic shutdown

REJECTION OF AUTHORITY
120. Withholding or withdrawal of allegiance

121. Refusal of public support
122. Literature and speeches advocating resistance

CITIZENS' NON-COOPERATION WITH GOVERNMENT

123. Boycott of legislative bodies
124. Boycott of elections
125. Boycott of government employment and positions
126. Boycott of government depts., agencies, and other bodies
127. Withdrawal from government educational institutions
128. Boycott of government-supported organizations
129. Refusal of assistance to enforcement agents
130. Removal of own signs and place-marks
131. Refusal to accept appointed officials
132. Refusal to dissolve existing institutions

CITIZENS' ALTERNATIVES TO OBEDIENCE

133. Reluctant and slow compliance
134. Non-obedience in absence of direct supervision
135. Popular non-obedience
136. Disguised disobedience
137. Refusal of an assemblage or meeting to disperse
138. Sit-down
139. Non-cooperation with conscription and deportation
140. Hiding, escape, and false identities
141. Civil disobedience of 'illegitimate' laws

ACTION BY GOVERNMENT PERSONNEL

142. Selective refusal of assistance by government aides

143. Blocking of lines of command and information
144. Stalling and obstruction
145. General administrative non-cooperation
146. Judicial non-cooperation
147. Deliberate inefficiency and selective non-cooperation by enforcement agents
148. Mutiny

DOMESTIC GOVERNMENTAL ACTION
149. Quasi-legal evasions and delays
150. Non-cooperation by constituent governmental units

INTERNATIONAL GOVERNMENTAL ACTION
151. Changes in diplomatic and other representations
152. Delay and cancellation of diplomatic events
153. Withholding of diplomatic recognition
154. Severance of diplomatic relations
155. Withdrawal from international organizations
156. Refusal of membership in international bodies
157. Expulsion from international organizations

Providing An Alternative, And Other Interventions

PSYCHOLOGICAL INTERVENTION
158. Self-exposure to the elements
159. The fast
    a) Fast of moral pressure

b) Hunger strike

c) Satyagrahic (Gandhian) fast

160. Reverse trial

161. Non-violent harassment

PHYSICAL INTERVENTION

162. Sit-in

163. Stand-in

164. Ride-in

165. Wade-in

166. Mill-in

167. Pray-in

168. Non-violent raids

169. Non-violent air raids

170. Non-violent invasion

171. Non-violent interjection

172. Non-violent obstruction

173. Non-violent occupation

SOCIAL INTERVENTION

174. Establishing new social patterns

175. Overloading of facilities

176. Stall-in

177. Speak-in

178. Guerilla theatre

179. Alternative social institutions

180. Alternative communication system

ECONOMIC INTERVENTION

181. Reverse strike
182. Stay-in strike
183. Non-violent land seizure
184. Defiance of blockades
185. Politically motivated counterfeiting
186. Preclusive purchasing
187. Seizure of assets
188. Dumping
189. Selective patronage
190. Alternative markets
191. Alternative transportation systems
192. Alternative economic institutions

POLITICAL INTERVENTION

193. Overloading of administrative systems
194. Disclosing identities of secret agents
195. Seeking imprisonment
196. Civil disobedience of 'neutral' laws
197. Work-on without collaboration
198. Dual sovereignty and parallel government

For further details, visit Sharp's Albert Einstein Foundation:
www.aeinstein.org.

Picture and Text Acknowledgements

The author and publisher would like to thank the following for permission to reproduce the images used in this book:

Page 10–11 Berlin wall © Caro / Alamy; Page 22–23 Manuscript illumination (detail), *The Legend of the Three Living and the Three Dead*, Ms.Arundel 83, fol.127 © akg-images / British Library; Page 27 Dog walker © Arnd Wiegmann / Reuters / Corbis; Page 30–31 Tank man © Jeff Widener / AP / Press Association Images; Page 42–43 Optimistic graffiti © Mario Tama / Getty Images; Page 69 Rosa Parks © Bettmann / Corbis; Page 78–79 Encouraging banner © Craftivist Collective and Robin Prime (photograph); Page 110 Ian Smith © Gamma-Keystone / Getty Images; Page 111 Robert Mugabe © Sipa Press / Rex Features; Page 125 Rob the rubbish man © Howard Barlow

All other images provided courtesy of the author.

Every effort has been made to contact the copyright holders of the material reproduced in this book. If any have been inadvertently overlooked the publisher will be pleased to make restitution at the earliest opportunity.

Pages 13 and 14 extracts are taken from *Mahatma Gandhi and Leo Tolstoy Letters*, Mahatma Gandhi (Long Beach Publications/ Navajivan Trust, 1987). Page 20 extract is taken from *How Are We*

To Live?, Peter Singer (Text Publishing, © Peter Singer, 1993). Page 26 extract is taken from *Man's Search for Meaning*, Victor Frankl (Beacon Press, 1946). Page 52 extract is taken from *Wild Swans*, Jung Chang (HarperCollins/Touchstone, © Jung Chang, 1991). Page 64 extract is taken from *Coming Back to Life*, Molly Young Brown and Joanna Macy (New Society Publishers, 1999). Page 67 extract is taken from *The Montgomery Bus Boycott And The Women Who Started It: The Memoir of Jo Ann Gibson Robinson*, ed. David J Garrow (University of Tennessee Press, 1987). Page 71 extract is reprinted from *In the Footsteps of Gandhi: Conversations with Spiritual Social Activists* (1990) by Catherine Ingram with permission of Parallax Press, Berkeley, California, USA, www.parallax.org

Notes